CITYSPOTS
LJUBI

Ryan Levitt

Written by Ryan Levitt
Original photography by Meghan Hurst
Front cover photography courtesy of Walter Bibikow/Getty Images
Series design based on an original concept by Studio 183 Limited

Produced by Cambridge Publishing Management Limited
Project Editor: Jenni Rainford
Layout: Paul Queripel
Maps: PC Graphics
Transport map: © Communicarta Limited

Published by Thomas Cook Publishing
A division of Thomas Cook Tour Operations Limited
Company Registration No. 1450464 England
PO Box 227, Unit 18, Coningsby Road
Peterborough PE3 8SB, United Kingdom
email: books@thomascook.com
www.thomascookpublishing.com
+ 44 (0) 1733 416477
ISBN-13: 978-1-84157-635-0
ISBN-10: 1-84157-635-2

First edition © 2006 Thomas Cook Publishing
Text © 2006 Thomas Cook Publishing
Maps © 2006 Thomas Cook Publishing
Series Editor: Kelly Anne Pipes
Project Editor: Ross Hilton
Production/DTP: Steven Collins

Printed and bound in Spain by GraphyCems

CONTENTS

SYMBOLS & ABBREVIATIONS

The following symbols are used throughout this book:

ⓐ address   ⓣ telephone   ⓕ fax   ⓔ email   ⓦ website address
ⓛ opening times   Ⓝ public transport connections   ⓘ important

The following symbols are used on the maps:

ℹ️ information office		○	city
✈ airport		○	large town
✚ hospital		○	small town
🛡 police station		=	motorway
🚌 bus station		—	main road
🚆 railway station		—	minor road
✝ cathedral		—	railway
❶ numbers denote featured cafés & restaurants			

Hotels and restaurants are graded by approximate price as follows:
£ budget   **££** mid-range   **£££** expensive

▶ *Take a trip on the tourist tram*

Introduction

While it may not be an influential capital like London, nor a sight-filled city like Paris, the Slovenian capital of Ljubljana is generating a lot of buzz among travellers, due to its streets of quaint charm, blossoming design and natural beauty. Low-cost airlines have blown the door wide open for holidaymakers searching for a city-break destination that combines affordability, intriguing history, great food and stunning surroundings. Ljubljana offers all this and more.

While shoppers may find the options a tad on the disappointing side, locals would never want you to spend your time exploring stuffy boutiques. Instead, they will point you to the banks of the Ljubljanica River, where residents enjoy nothing more than a leisurely stroll as they watch the water flow by.

A visit to Ljubljana is made for those who want to relax. You won't need any strict itineraries or tight transport schedules to get the most out of your stay, as the city is so compact. To go from one end of Ljubljana to the other should take you no more than 45 minutes on foot – and that's if you walk at a slow pace.

Don't be at all worried that the small size might translate into a boring time – Slovenians are some of the friendliest and most welcoming on the continent. If they think you're looking a bit down-hearted, they'll be sure to invite you to join their group in order to ensure that you experience a bit of true local hospitality.

Lovers of the great outdoors are especially well catered for, as Ljubljana is surrounded by huge tracts of untouched land. A large chunk of the western half of the city is devoted to the paths and fields of Tivoli park, while a mere hour outside town will take you to anything from the Alps to a fairytale lake complete with a castle overlooking its banks.

Ljubljana might be hard to say, but with all these options, your travel agent is sure to get used to saying its name as you book your stay again and again. Start saving your tolars today!

⬧ *Each new twist and turn offers an enchanting vista*

When to go

Ljubljana is worth visiting at any time of year. For many, the city really comes alive in the summer, when one outdoor event follows the next, whether it is a colourful parade, street festival or an open-air concert. If what goes on in the city itself is not enough, then head off into the surroundings: the lake and castle of Bled, the seafront at Piran, the fresh air of the Julian Alps are all enticing.

SEASONS & CLIMATE

Ljubljana has a continental climate, hot in summer and cold in winter. From November to March the city often ices over, with spring thawing everything out some time in late March/early April. Though the atmosphere is often quite damp, the temperatures are pleasant enough to allow outdoor activities such as walking and cycling.

Summers can be hot and muggy, and at this time of the year, the locals flock to the shade of Tivoli or nearby Lake Bled. In early autumn, temperatures are still very mild and, like spring, this is a good time to explore the city's streets. In winter, temperatures can drop fast and sudden snowstorms occasionally occur. Wrap up warm, and the bars of the city are sure to heat any chill.

ANNUAL EVENTS

In Ljubljana, and Slovenia in general, there are many more events than can be mentioned here. The tourist offices in Ljubljana and the various regional capitals can provide a list of events. Also note that exact dates may change from year to year – check first. There is a comprehensive calendar of events at ⓦ www.ljubljana-tourism.si/en

---

◑ *During a festival is an excellent time to visit*

Festival
Ljubljana 2005

www.festival-lj.si

June

International Biennial of Graphic Arts Held on odd-numbered years at the International Centre of Graphic Arts from mid-June to mid-September, this celebration of design is slowly gaining in prestige among members of the global art community. ⓦ www.mglc-lj.org

June–September

Ljubljana Festival International music, theatre and dance performances. ⓦ www.ljubljanafestival.si

October

City of Women Art and culture created by women are the focus of this international festival of contemporary arts. ⓦ www.cityofwomen-a.si

Ljubljana Marathon This marathon was begun in 1996 and continues to draw a better class of athlete each time it is run.

December

Christmas concerts Popular with locals throughout the country. For a truly special experience, try and get tickets to the spectacular concert held in the caves at Postojna about 60 minutes southwest of the capital.

New Year's Eve Ljubljana's New Year's Eve party. Local residents congregate at Prešernov trg to take part in the celebrations.

Outside Ljubljana

As Slovenia is so small, events in other parts of the country still generate much interest amongst residents of the capital. Some of the higher-profile events to consider include:

Women's World Cup, Pohorje Slovenia is the land that brought the world the sport of skiing. See the finest ladies in the world go for a place on the podium at this major stop on the World Cup circuit, held every January.

Kurentovanje, Ptuj This annual 'rite of spring' is held in the historic town of Ptuj every February. Celebrations last for the ten days leading up to Shrove Tuesday and are the biggest Mardi Gras celebrations in the country.

Rock Otočec, Novo Mesto Slovenia's largest open-air rock concert lasts for three days in early July and acts as the national version of Glastonbury. Prečna airfield, northwest of Nove Mesto, is transformed into a music-lover's paradise. Just don't forget to pack your toilet paper.

Cow's Ball, Bohinj Probably Slovenia's wackiest event is this weekend festival held in the town of Bohinj every September. Folk dance, food, drink and music celebrate the return of the cows from their high pastures to the valleys.

PUBLIC HOLIDAYS
New Year's holidays 1 & 2 January
Prešeren Day (Slovenian Culture Day) 8 February
Easter Sunday & Monday Late March/Early April
Insurrection Day 27 April
Labour Day holidays 1 & 2 May
National Day 25 June
Assumption Day 15 August
Reformation Day 31 October
All Saints' Day 1 November
Christmas Day 25 December
Independence Day 26 December

The city of summer festivals

As soon as the sun begins to shine, residents of Ljubljana come out to play. The Slovenian capital is a city of summer festivals dedicated to showcasing everything from large-scale theatre to intimate musical performances. Kicking off the summer season is Druga Godba Ljubljana, held at the end of May for one week every year. This celebration highlights the sights and sounds of Slovenian and international alternative/world music artists. This is definitely the best opportunity to experience and enjoy Slovenian folk and traditional music. One of the most enjoyable festivals is the Ana Desetnica Street Theatre festival, which is held at the end of June. This colourful collection of performances takes over the Old Town and highlights acts of magic and music, often with a 'busker' feel.

Also at the end of June is the annual Ljubljana Jazz Festival. World-class musicians are often included on the bill of this three-day celebration of jazz and urban music.

From June to the middle of September is the Ljubljana Summer Festival. This is the festival of choice for fans of high art, as the city swarms with opera, ballet, theatre and classical music. Performances are often programmed in unlikely venues, which often prove to be inspiring.

Finally, the last festival of the summer season is TrnFest Ljubljana in August. More hands-on than other festivals, this hot-ticket event offers up workshops, guest lectures, small-scale performance and exhibitions organised by the KUD cultural centre. Families should note that some of the performances are specifically designed with kids in mind.

Just an hour outside the town is the lakeside community of Bled, home to a weekend craft fair and fireworks display known as Bled

Days in mid-July. While not in Ljubljana, so many locals go that you'll probably feel as if you're in the middle of the city anyway.

For something more authentic, travel instead to the more unspoilt countryside towns such as Ptuj in the east of the country. Here is where you will find regular harvest celebrations and 'Medieval' reconstructions that feel truly Slovenian.

🔺 *Throngs of visitors gather in the market square during performances*

History

Ljubljana's history dates back to the Bronze Age. Inhabitants lived peacefully during these early days until the Celts moved southwards towards the Balkans from what is now France, Germany and the Czech Republic around 400 BC. The Roman Empire took over in 181 BC and established a number of regional colonies in order to ensure control over the area. Roman power was maintained until the 5th century AD when the Huns took advantage of the destruction of the Roman Empire.

The first Slavs to arrive in Slovenia came from the Carpathian basin and settled in the 6th century in the river valleys of Sava, Drava and Mura. These are the ancestors of today's Slovenians; however, the term 'Slovenian' didn't come into regular use until the 18th century.

Over the next 500 years, various clans, including the Franks, Magyars and Germans, ruled over the country, eventually culminating in the rise of the Habsburg family during the early Middle Ages. The Habsburgs ruled over Slovenia with an iron fist from the 14th century until the end of World War I. The laws of the land were administered by parliaments of princes, feudal lords and town representatives until the 17th century – however, all decisions needed to be approved by the Habsburgs.

Peasant uprisings caused problems for the Habsburgs at various times between the 14th and 19th centuries, as the gulf between the rich and poor continued to widen. Attacks from the south by Ottoman Turks fuelled rebellion as Slovenes were often left to fend for themselves during the deadly battles.

Protestantism entered the country as the Reformation swept across Europe. Determined to squash the revolutionary concepts introduced by this new branch of Christianity, the resident Catholic princes banished any believers from the country. This law didn't last long as state coffers began to reach breaking point. The Habsburgs battled to boost finances following years of ill-fated wars in other parts of the Empire. Roads were built, freedom of religion was re-introduced and corrupt Catholic orders were abolished.

The arrival of Napoleon brought new-found hope to Slovenia and initiated a period of Romantic Nationalism that would not be seen again until the independence movement of the early 1990s. The French general imposed a number of new reforms and allowed Slovene to be used in schools for the first time. These glory days didn't last for long as Austrian rule and the harsh feudal system were reintroduced in 1814.

World War I was the final nail in the coffin of Austrian rule. When the war ended, Slovenes joined together with Serbs and Croats to form the Independent Kingdom of Serbs, Croats and Slovenes. This unity was fragile, and faced ever stronger struggles following the introduction of Communism post-World War II. Were it not for the strong (if not dictatorial) rule of Tito, socialist Yugoslavia would never have survived. Finally, in 1991 after years of struggle and three days battling Yugoslav forces, Slovenia gained independence for the first time in its history. The country became a full member of the EU in May 2004.

Lifestyle

Slovenia has a reputation for efficiency that is almost Germanic in flavour. Luckily, the Slavic and Balkan blood provides a streak of humour that translates into a very warm welcome any time you are introduced.

● Prešernov trg is the city's main square

Residents are good business people and hard workers. The country was really the only one to emerge from the break-up of Yugoslavia relatively unscathed – primarily due to the nation's history as the region's financial hub.

Locals love a good time and have plenty of opportunities to indulge. While strong for the Balkans, the local economy isn't particularly booming, causing most residents to budget wisely. Inflation is a real problem and is actually the one thing standing between the country and the adoption of the euro. Admission costs to hip nightclubs are half those you'd expect in other major cities and drink prices are affordable. Speaking of nights out, a typical evening will start late: most clubs don't even open their doors until 23.00, and the funky and fashionable leave it another two hours before they even consider going inside. Bars are open (almost) all hours. Walk through most neighbourhoods and it is perfectly possible to find a bar open as late as 06.00. Locals enjoy a leisurely drinking culture and the company of friends.

Though there is a lack of big business in Ljubljana, this is starting to change as the city emerges as the powerhouse of the Balkans. A strong and individual community spirit survives as the city's biggest employers continue to be sole proprietorships and independent companies. When someone says they work for a family-owned company in Ljubljana, that family has most likely owned the company for many generations.

Shopping isn't the all-consuming practice found in Paris, London or New York. Hours reflect this trend, as the bulk of shops remain closed on Sundays and have severely restricted hours on Saturdays. Instead, it's a beer and a gossip that residents enjoy the most – preferably at an outdoor café on a warm summer evening. Winters can be harsh and locals value every minute of good weather.

Culture

Ljubljana loves its artistic institutions. Public and private funding supports a number of theatres, concert halls, opera and ballet houses – both traditional and cutting-edge. Attendance at the various open-air theatres and concert venues explodes during the summer, when the city offers up a new festival almost every week – with most performances free of charge and open to all.

In warmer months, Prešenova trg is the place to go to enjoy live performance, whether in the form of rock acts, live swing bands, buskers or mimes. For a few tolar more, then walk a few blocks west to the Cankarjev Dom. This is the main performance venue in the city for big-name rock and classical acts. Acoustics are said to be superb. Philharmonic Hall is another venue worth booking tickets at, especially if the Slovenian Philharmonic Orchestra is scheduled to perform. The orchestra is one of the oldest in the world, was once conducted by the composer Gustav Mahler (during the 1881–2 season) and continues to be widely respected. The Slovenian Chamber Choir also calls this venue home.

Diverse offerings can be found at the Križanke arts complex – a collection of open-air and intimate theatres housed in a converted 18th-century monastery. The grounds are also the headquarters of the annual Ljubljana Summer Festival.

Squats and independent community centres are still widely accepted in Ljubljana, with local artists famous for transforming disused buildings into arts complexes, discos, bars and hostels. The most famous example of this is found at Metelkova and the Hostel

● *This statue stands proudly in Piran main square*

Celica, where a former army barracks has been completely repainted and redesigned.

So why is Ljubljana so artistic? The country's status as a regional economic powerhouse provides one answer, especially when combined with new-found independence. For many years, the idea of a Slovenian identity was buried under layers of communism and Yugoslavian nationalism. Once independence was achieved, leaders realised that Slovenians needed to determine their identity and ask questions by using the arts as a medium. Government support is therefore high.

The two fields that remain relatively untapped are modern music and literature. Few musicians, bands or writers have reached any form of success outside national borders, with the exception of the poet France Prešeren – and his success dates back to the early 19th century.

Artistic work is rarely translated from its original Slovenian, which perhaps explains the relative obscurity of many of the country's most celebrated modern talents. The fact that the country is the third-smallest market for literature in Europe doesn't help matters much. In this country, selling 500 copies of a book will get you on the bestseller list.

Locally produced television and film aren't very successful either. As most residents speak English and the quality of Slovenian-produced television is so poor, there are few reasons to watch it. Independence may have provided Slovenia with a proud, new identity – but it has also limited the market to which artists can showcase their work. Success will only come with exposure, and further entrenchment into the European Common Market.

❿ *A bustling market square*

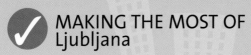

Shopping

Despite the fact that Ljubljana is a European capital, shopping options aren't all that spectacular. Locals aren't known for their sense of style, with many limiting their purchases to the chain stores and bland ready-to-wear found in the BTC City Shopping Centre. Visitors considering Ljubljana for a shopping-filled short break may want to think twice. Shops close firmly at 13.00 on Saturday afternoons and don't even think about re-opening until Monday morning. There are calls for these hours to change in the near future, but a recent referendum was unsuccessful.

Better possibilities lie tucked away in the side streets of the Left Bank and Old Town, which provide a mixed bag of tourist traps and local designer boutiques. Local design work tends to be stylish, sleek and affordable when compared with similar products in Paris and London. They won't, however, be particularly adventurous. The best bet for items of originality can be found every day in the stalls of the Central Market. Other markets worth browsing through are the Antiques Flea Market held every Sunday from 08.00–13.00 and the arts and crafts market open every Friday from 08.00–15.00 near the Cathedral. Summers also introduce a weekly art market by the name of Ljubljana Montmartre into the mix of shopping suggestions. Paintings and ceramics go on sale every Saturday between June and September from 09.00–16.00.

Slovenian souvenirs are available in shops all over Ljubljana; however, most items associated with Slovenia are actually produced regionally, outside of the city. If you are planning an extensive tour of the country, save your purchases of arts and crafts until you visit the region in which the items are famous. Purchases to consider include fine lace, bottles of brandy and wine, black pottery, glassware, beehive panels and honey.

Antiques, especially from the art nouveau period, are great purchases in the city. There are a number of boutiques that specialise in the period – all featuring well-maintained and/or restored items for fans of this decorating era. Shipping is easy to arrange and can often be negotiated at very advantageous rates.

USEFUL SHOPPING PHRASES

What time do the shops open/close?
Ob kateri uri se zaprejo odprejo/trgovine?
Ob kateree ooree seh zapreyo od-preh-yoh/trhgoveeneh?

How much is this?
Koliko stane tole?
Koleeko staneh toleh?

Can I try this on?
Lahko tole pomerim?
Lakhko toleh pomereem?

My size is ...
Nosim številko ...
Noseem shteveelko ...

I'll take this one, thank you
Tega bi vzel(a), prosim
Tega bee oozel(a) prosseem

**This is too large/too small/too expensive.
Do you have any others?**
Tole je preveliko/premajhno/predrago. Imate še kaj drugega?
Toleh yeh preveleeko/premaykhno/predrago. Eemateh sheh kay droogega?

Eating & drinking

Ljubljana is beginning to offer more than just Slovenian cuisine on city menus – but it's been a long time coming. The country doesn't have a large immigrant population – and therefore doesn't have a wealth of cuisines it can offer visitors. If you say 'foreign food' to a Slovenian, they'll most likely point you in the direction of a local pizzeria (although judging by the number of pizzerias in Slovenia, it could be argued that Italy actually stole this favourite menu item from Slovenians).

Traditional restaurants remain popular and usually fall into two categories: tourist-oriented eateries featuring Slovenian *gostilne*-style architecture and servers clad in local costume, or hole-in-the-wall establishments with hearty patrons and even heartier (and heavier) dishes. In either case, the meal is sure to be lip-smackingly good.

Recent imports, including a wave of Mexican establishments and a Chinese takeaway, are beginning to make inroads into the Ljubljana dining scene, but quality tends to vary (along with the authenticity of the dishes). Outside of Ljubljana, you will be restricted to Slovenian establishments and pizzerias.

Vegetarians beware! Always check with the establishment to see if a dish is truly meat-free. In many cases, locals will think that chicken and ham don't count as meat.

PRICE RATING

The restaurant price guides indicate the approximate cost of a three-course meal for one person, excluding drinks, at the time of writing.

£ up to €10; ££ between €10 and €20; £££ above €20

EATING

Every meal in Slovenia will be accompanied by bread. On a gluten-free diet? You'll have to break it during your stay – especially when faced with the variety of doughy treats on offer. Specialities include wholewheat bread and 'mottled' bread made from three different types of dough (buckwheat, wheat and corn). For a real treat, be sure to try the braided Christmas loaves available throughout the city during the run-up to the holiday.

Another filling Slovenian option is groats. Made from barley, buckwheat or corn, these dense 'porridges' are often served with a savoury side dish such as pork crackling. Definitely not for those looking to lose weight.

No meal is complete for a Slovenian unless it includes meat. The most commonly served are veal, beef, game and, above all, pork. Chicken and goose are rarely dished up. Also popular are fish and shellfish, even in mountainous regions. Trout caught in the Soča River is especially valued.

Before the main course is presented, diners often start with a bowl of soup. This is usually made from chicken or beef broth with

⬤ Take time out for a coffee or a horse-meat sandwich

an added dash of small egg noodles. In winter, soups can be much thicker and include potatoes, beans, smoked pork, sausage or sauerkraut. These traditional potages were designed as a filling, warm dish to help alleviate hunger and banish the cold during the long winter months.

Locals can often be found snacking on Slovenian dessert delicacies. The most common choice is *potica*, a kind of nut roll eaten during the day with coffee or tea, although other varieties filled with poppy seeds, walnuts, sultanas and apples are also as popular.

Find yourself stuck for a snack? You won't be for long, considering the sheer number of food stands dotted throughout the city. The two most common are *burek*, which is a kind of flaky pastry filled with cheese and mince, and 'horse-meat sandwiches', which are exactly what they sound like – large sandwiches filled with horse meat.

DRINKING

Be sure to try the delicious bottles of Slovenian wine. The country has been making wine since the days of the Roman Empire – and most of the best varieties never even leave the country.

Many visitors think that the best wine comes from the Primorska region, which is famous for producing strong, fiery reds. Others prefer the dry, light reds found in the region of Posavje, which runs across the Sava River from eastern Štajerska. All of Slovenia's 14 wine regions boast an official wine route – so if you have particular interest, be sure to inquire about maps and trails at the Tourist Information Centre of the region you are hoping to visit.

Other drinks worth trying out are locally produced beers, ciders and a sort of honeyed brandy served straight from the fridge during the summer months.

USEFUL DINING PHRASES

I would like a table for ... people
Rad(a) bi mizo za ...
Rad(a) bee meezo za ...

May I have the bill, please?
Račun, prosim?
Rachoon prosseem?

Could I have it well-cooked/medium/rare, please?
Rad(a) bi dobro/pečen zrezek/zrezek po angleško?
Rad(a) bee dobro/pechen zrezek/zrezek po angleshko?

I am a vegetarian. Does this contain meat?
Vegetarijanec sem/Vegetarijanka sem. (*fem.*) Ali ta jed
vsebuje meso?
*Veh-geh-tar-yahnets sehm/Veh-geh-tar-yahn-kah sehm. Ah-lee
tah yed vseh-boo-yeh meh-saw?*

Where is the toilet (restroom) please?
Oprostite, kje je stranišče (toaleta)?
Oprossteeteh, kyeh yeh straneeshcheh (toaleta)?

I would like a cup of/two cups of/another coffee/tea
Kavo/čaj, prosim. Dve kavi/dva čaja, prosim. Se eno kavo/še en
čaj, prosim
*Kavo/chay prosseem. Dve kavee/dva chaya, prosseem. Sheh eno
kavo/sheh en chay, prosseem*

Entertainment & nightlife

When it comes to life after dark, Ljubljana isn't exactly packed with options. While a blossoming alternative scene is beginning to emerge and the effect of a dedication towards design is taking shape, the city's population just isn't large enough to support a diverse scene.

Ljubljana's youth tend to dictate the types of activities a visitor might find there. The former squats of Metelkova and converted barracks at the Celica Hostel attract a bohemian crowd. This is the place to go if you like your clubs rough, ready, adventurous and welcoming. Designer labels certainly aren't de rigueur.

The Left Bank, particularly the streets around the 'Centre' district, hosts a wide range of high-end, well-respected cultural institutions including the Philharmonic Orchestra, National Theatre, Opera and Ballet. While performances do draw a well-bred crowd, they certainly aren't as stuffy as productions in nearby Austria or Italy. They still shouldn't be a place to wear your new trainers, however. What might be pennies for you is a fortune for most locals. Many will have saved up long and hard for a ticket.

Closer to the river is where the city's best cafés and restaurants can be found. Knafijev prehod is a pedestrianised street upon which many atmospheric bars and eateries can be found. On warm nights, these venues positively heave with both locals and visitors. Many will offer outdoor tables so you can make the most of the weather and enjoy Slovenia's favourite pastime – people-watching.

Summer is a time of festivals and Slovenians always love a good performance, especially when it's free. At various times throughout the season, Prešernov trg and the Križanke cultural complex are transformed into free performance venues complete with live musicians and dance. You may not have heard of any of the players, but all the world will be a stage when you join the masses as they dance and sing along with the performers.

⬥ *Street entertainment is free for all*

As Krakovo and Trnovo are very residential, bars and clubs in this district are extremely welcoming. You'll invariably be greeted warmly at any of the venues in these neighbourhoods, making them great regions to explore if you're visiting Ljubljana on your own. These neighbourhoods remain the district of choice for artists, students and squatters due to the proximity to the Ljubljana University. Students also bring a bit of a late-night vibe to the area, making it one of the only neighbourhoods (other than the area around the bus station) where you are guaranteed to find a bite of *burek* throughout the evening.

The bar scene, thanks to votes of confidence from a number of style bibles, is starting to heat up. Most of the newest venues have a less is more mentality, preferring minimalism and modernism when designing interiors. These drinking dens are great if you want to surround yourself with a stylish crowd, but aren't that great if you're looking to meet locals as patrons usually keep to their individual groups.

Clubbers don't really have much of a choice in Ljubljana. Aside from the previously mentioned Metelkova complex, the most popular locations for a night of dancing are the Bacchus Centre Club and Funfactory. These multi-level, multi-venue centres of pleasure offer everything from techno to rock. Don't expect anything that sways too far from a Eurotrash beat. International DJs sometimes make an appearance.

Finally, for a bit of Latin rhythm, head over to the Casa del Papa restaurant and its sister venues, the Cuban Room (for salsa dancing and music) and the Key West Bar (for smooth cigars and even smoother cocktails).

▶ *Night time along the banks of the Ljubljanica River*

Sport & relaxation

Slovenians love the great outdoors and will trek, hike, bike or walk as often as they possibly can. Winters can be long and hard, but it doesn't stop locals from keeping fit and healthy. Fitness centres are dotted throughout the city, though most locals prefer to keep fit by incorporating exercise into their daily lives, rather than sweat in an airless room. If you must continue your prescribed fitness routine, most hotels of at least three-star quality will offer basic facilities, including cardio and weight machines.

Tivoli Recreation Centre Fitness centre with an indoor swimming pool, tennis courts, roller-skating rink, ice rink and sauna. ⓐ Celovška cesta 25 ❶ 01 431 5155 ⓛ 08.00–20.00 Mon–Sun

As the city is situated on a relatively flat plain, opportunities to enjoy mountain sports are limited unless you go an hour north to Bled and beyond into the Julian Alps. For that, locals hop on a bus. Weekends are extremely busy. Residents also take advantage of the large green space of Tivoli that is situated in the west of the city. In fact, it is perfectly possible to take part in a spot of cross-country skiing on Tivoli's trails. Alternatively, rent a bicycle to explore the city's highways and byways, including the park's designated paths.

Tivoli was built for the local populace in the early 19th century. In the summer, the massive green space positively buzzes with activity. At all hours of the day, you will spot joggers, picnickers, families, Frisbee throwers and office workers basking in the sun. As the park is so large (or at least large for Ljubljana at 5 sq km/2 sq miles), it is perfectly possible to wander off the paths into hidden, tree-covered corners that feel like something straight out of a fairy tale.

Gentle activity is also performed in the form of walking and promenading. During the summer a stroll up and down the banks of the Ljubljanica River is considered the height of fashion. Most will traverse the stretch between the Dragon and Cobbler's Bridge. Adventurous souls can, however, continue on until they reach the Trnovo Bridge before they turn back to the city centre.

▲ *Tivoli Park*

Accommodation

Slovenia's new status as a chic city-break destination is a bonus for travellers. Never before has there been so much selection in terms of quality and quantity. Unfortunately, there is still a dearth of quality city-centre hotels and prices remain high. If you don't book in advance you could find yourself out of luck in your search for a hotel room – both during the week and on weekends. Be sure to check the event calendar on the Ljubljana Tourist Information Centre website well in advance of your planned stay.

Those who like their hotels with a bit more character won't be disappointed. Renovations, restorations and rebuilds have created new properties, including antique-packed salutes to art nouveau, sleek and chic boutique properties, and grande dame hotels featuring restored interiors. The city outskirts, while inconvenient geographically, offer some great bargains for fans of modern minimalism, while the streets around Prešeren Square feature four- and five-star historic hotels. Finally, for those on a budget, Ljubljana's hostels are an excellent choice. Not only are prices reasonable, they are probably the most well-maintained and most character-filled dorm rooms and beds in Europe. One of them is even in a former army prison!

PRICE RATINGS

Hotels in Slovenia are graded according to a voluntary star system, running from one star for a cheap guesthouse to five stars for a luxurious property with numerous facilities. The ratings in this book are as follows:

£ up to €80; ££ €80–140; £££ over €140

All prices are for a single night in a double room/two people.

HOTELS

Park Hotel £–££ In the event the Celica is full, this budget hotel is a good option. While the hotel is located in an uninviting concrete tower, rooms are comfortable (if a little basic). ⓐ Tabor 9 ⓣ 01 433 1306 ⓦ www.hotelpark.si

City Hotel Turist ££ Quality three-star hotel designed for business travellers. Rooms are ensuite and air-conditioned. On-street parking and cycle hire are available. Comfortable, secure, though lacking any real character. ⓐ Dalmatinova 15 ⓣ 01 234 9130 ⓦ www.hotelturist.si

Domina Grand Media Ljubljana ££ This hi-tech property was opened in summer 2004 to great acclaim. Rooms feature massive plasma-screen TVs, virtual sightseeing tours of the city and broadband internet access. Other facilities include an indoor pool, saunas, gym and full-scale casino. While it's located 3 km (2 miles) from the city centre, a regular hotel shuttle bus is available to take guests to and from Prešeren Square. ⓐ Dunajska 160 ⓣ 01 569 1192 ⓦ www.dominahotels.it

Mons Hotel ££ This chic design hotel was opened in September 2004 and features stylish green glass walls that bathe the hotel in light. While the location is good for business travellers, holidaymakers will need a taxi to get anywhere central. ⓐ Pot za Brdom 55 ⓣ 01 470 2700 ⓦ www.hotel.mons.si

Grand Hotel Union Business ££–£££ This modern hotel is a wing of the historic Grand Hotel Union located next door. While the exterior isn't as inspiring as its more famous neighbour, the interiors are almost exactly the same and guests can use all of the original's facilities. ⓐ Miklošičeva 3 ⓣ 01 308 1170 ⓦ www.gh-union.si

Grand Hotel Union Garni ££–£££ Centrally located and recently renovated, this modern hotel is convenient and comfortable. While the Business should be your first choice, the Garni is a nice second option. ⓐ Miklošičeva 9 ⓣ 01 308 4300 ⓦ www.gh-union.si

Slon Best Western Premier ££–£££ Shoppers rejoice at the location of this great hotel in the middle of Slovenska. The hotel is named 'elephant' in honour of Emperor Maximilian, who is once thought to have camped elephants on this site during his stay in the city. For good rates, check out the Best Western website in advance of your stay. ⓐ Slovenska 34 ⓣ 01 470 1100 ⓦ www.hotelslon.com

Grand Hotel Union Executive £££ Beautiful art nouveau grande dame hotel considered to be the finest in town. Located just a short stroll from Prešeren Square and the river, it's convenient to the entire city. Rooms are classically designed (if a little uninspired). Higher floors provide the best views. Book ahead to ensure you get a room. ⓐ Miklošičeva 1 ⓣ 01 308 1270 ⓦ www.gh-union.si

Lev Hotel £££ This modern hotel is the city's only five-star property. Designed with the business traveller in mind, it lacks a little in luxury considering the price. Rooms are spacious, if a bit bland – but the facilities are top-notch. Try to get a city-side room for views of the castle and Old Town. ⓐ Vošnjakova 1 ⓣ 01 433 2155 ⓦ www.hotel-lev.si

---

▶ *An abundance of art nouveau architecture*

GUESTHOUSES

Pension Pri Mraku £–££ This old-world guesthouse is designed with a bohemian feel, complete with old-fashioned draperies using luxurious fabrics. Located close to the Križanke theatre, it's a good place for culture vultures to rest their head. ⓐ Rimska 4 ⓣ 01 421 9600 ⓦ www.daj-dam.si

HOSTELS & CAMPSITES

Celica Hostel £ These converted military barracks are now one of the hottest places to stay in town. Constantly sold out, the Celica offers rooms of 2, 3, 4, 5, 7 and 14 beds. Each room has been designed by a different local artist, with results varying from austere simplicity to overwhelmingly colourful. Smaller rooms require you to share bathroom facilities, while rooms of four or more people offer en-suite toilets and showers. There is a room for disabled guests on the ground floor. At night, the place is hopping with hip 20- and 30-somethings drawn by the Arabic-inspired bar, tasty restaurant and cheap internet access.

If you need your sleep, Celica may not be the place for you. The floors echo, so even a simple whisper can sound deafening. The neighbouring Metelkova squat is also extremely loud, often until the small hours of the morning. From the Celica, it's about a 15-minute walk to the city centre. Advance bookings are essential. ⓐ Metelkova 9 ⓣ 01 430 1890 ⓦ www.souhostel.si

Youth Hostel Ljubljana Tabor £ These student dorms are only available during school holidays between late June and late August. Accommodation is available in single, twin, triple and quad-bed rooms. ⓐ Vidovdanska 7 ⓣ 01 234 8840 ⓦ www.youth-hostel.si

ⓞ *A room at the Celica Hostel*

THE BEST OF LJUBLJANA

Ljubljana is ideal for a short weekend break, because it's easy to get around. Explore the Old City for history, the Left Bank for culture, Krakovo and Trnovo for community, or Tivoli for outdoor pursuits. For daytrip suggestions, see pages 42–43.

TOP 10 ATTRACTIONS

- **Ljubljana Castle** This hilltop castle provides breathtaking views over the city as far as the Julian Alps. Don't miss the multimedia movie, shown at the base of the tower (see page 65)

- **Prešernov Trg** Ljubljana's main square always buzzes with activity. Approach it from the Triple Bridge to enjoy the best in local architecture (see page 74)

- **Ljubljanica River** The river is Ljubljana's heart. During summer months, the banks are packed with couples, friends, families and visitors. Pull up a chair at one of the cafés and watch the world pass by (see page 44)

- **Tivoli** Get away from the hustle and bustle of city life in Ljubljana's urban park paradise (see page 92)

- **Celica Hostel and Metelkova** Local bohemians hang out at these restored and renovated army buildings that have been taken over by local artists. A great place to mix with the local in-crowd (see pages 38 & 80)

- **Central Market** Stalls and shops run by local farmers and artisans, selling crafts and fresh produce (see page 66)

- **Križanke** Explore this cultural centre that was once home to a large monastery (see page 81)

- **Slovenska** Time for shopping! Great boutiques and designer goodies await you on this main artery (see page 77)

- **Narodni Muzej Slovenije (National Museum of Slovenia)** Slovenia's largest and most extensive museum holds a treasure trove of artefacts (see page 75)

- **Bled** Just an hour outside of town is Ljubljana's favourite rural retreat. Go for a day or a week – there's plenty to see, do and enjoy (see page 102)

▼ *Cycle your way to the harbour*

Here is an at-a-glance guide to seeing the best that Ljubljana has to offer, depending on how much time you have.

HALF-DAY: LJUBLJANA IN A HURRY

It's easy to see the bulk of the city's biggest sites in just a few hours. Start your day at the Ljubljana Castle by taking the train from Prešernov trg. Trains leave hourly, so check the schedule before planning your day. Explore the castle grounds, being sure not to miss going up the tower, and then follow Študentovska as it snakes down to Vodnikov trg. From here, it's just steps away to the Central Market with its wares of goodies, ending up at Dragon Bridge, just north of the Tourist Information Centre.

1 DAY: TIME TO SEE A LITTLE MORE

Follow the itinerary marked above and continue your explorations of the Old Town by following the river along the riverside path. Pass the Triple Bridge (on your right) and the river will begin to bend to the left. Enjoy the walk along the road, also known as Cankarjevo Nabrežje, being sure to delve away from the river to enjoy the small, character-filled side streets.

2–3 DAYS: SHORT CITY-BREAK

With two or three days you can get a much better impression of what the city has to offer. Take the recommended tour for day one. Follow this with explorations of Tivoli, including cycling along the various park paths. On day three, choose a walk around the museums in the far west of the neighbourhood known as Centre. Alternatively, head down to Krakovo and Trnovo to visit these creative communities.

LONGER: ENJOYING LJUBLJANA TO THE FULL

Get more out of Ljubljana by getting out of town. A visit to Bled will afford you lakeside splendour, while Piran provides a jewel of a seaside destination. Both destinations will provide memories that you will treasure.

● *Lake Bled is a popular trip from the capital*

Something for nothing

Some of Slovenia's best sights are absolutely free. Locals aren't rich and they have mastered the art of having a good time for very little money. One of the most treasured experiences is a simple stroll along the banks of the Ljubljanica River. While the cafés will do their best to help part you from your money, there is no need to sit down at one of the tables. Instead, just walk along the riverfront from the Dragon Bridge to as far as the Trnovo Bridge. In fact, the bridges of Ljubljana are some of the most treasured sights in the city, particularly the graceful sweep of the Triple Bridge designed by Jože Plečnik. For just a few tolar more, you can even splurge on a delicious cone of gelato.

Speaking of Plečnik, architecture is one of the main draws of the Slovenian capital. The city is packed with art nouveau treasures and there are plenty of opportunities to see these beautiful examples of design, particularly along Miklošičeva Cesta. Prime possibilities include the exteriors of the Grand Union Hotel, the Cooperative Bank and the People's Loan Bank.

Another cheap and cheerful option is a walk through Tivoli. This large park is a popular place for a picnic or kickabout with friends. Bikes can be rented for very little if you want to enjoy the network of paths. Alternatively, just explore the various fields and hills.

Many of Ljubljana's smaller museums are free of charge, including the Brewery Museum, DESSA Architectural Gallery, Tobacco Museum and Slovenian School Museum. While the collections aren't as filled with 'wow' factor as some of the other galleries in the city, they all exhibit wonderful slices of Slovenian life you might not find elsewhere.

Finally, if you want to see the big sights and save money, consider purchasing the Ljubljana Card at the Tourist Information Centre.

This discount card provides money off admission fees, cafés, club entrance charges and hotel accommodation, restaurant meals, shops, for a period of 72 hours. Free bus transportation is also included in the price of the card, which costs 3000SIT.

⬤ *The city's abundant art nouveau architecture is free for all to enjoy*

When it rains

Ljubljana can be a bit of a challenge when the weather turns. One of the best things to do if the clouds look a little grey is to head for the museums located in and around Prešernova in the west end of Centre. The collections on display at the Museum of Modern Art,

◒ The Postojna Caves are great for exploring

National Gallery and National Museum of Slovenia are extensive enough to warrant hours, if not a full day, of exploration – a perfect option to help pass a rainy day.

Another possibility – and one that children will probably find more interesting – is to head out of town to the Postojna Caves. By bus, the Postojna Caves are about one hour away from Ljubljana, and offer plenty of fascinating opportunities for both kids and adults.

Visitors book themselves onto 1½-hour tours that take them 1,700 m (5,577 ft) into the cave system by train before walking along a prescribed route past the Big Mountain, along the Russian Bridge and into the Concert Hall. Along the way, you will see fantastic stalagmites, stalactites, curtains of rock formation and columns. Just before reaching the concert hall, there is a small tank filled with four examples of the legendary 'human fish' or *Proteus anguinus*. Sometimes mistaken by locals for baby dragons, this blind salamander is native to the cave system and can breathe both in and out of water.

No matter what the weather might be like outside, the temperature inside remains a constant 10°C with 95 per cent humidity. Depending on your tolerance for cold weather, you may want to consider renting one of the felt jackets available at the beginning of the tour.

Finally, if you want to shop till you drop, then the best option is to take a taxi out to the BTC City shopping centre. While this centre offers a wide selection of shops, the actual walkways between each shop aren't covered – so it's a good idea to wear a coat. If unique wares are what you're looking for, then don't bother planning a visit. With few exceptions, most of the brands are the usual high-street names that you'll be used to back home.

On arrival

TIME DIFFERENCES

Slovenian clocks follow Central European Time (CET). During
Daylight Saving Time (end Mar–end Oct), the clocks are put ahead
by one hour. In the Slovenian summer, at 12.00, time elsewhere is
as follows:

Australia Eastern Standard Time 20.00, Central Standard Time 19.30,
Western Standard Time 18.00
New Zealand 22.00
South Africa 12.00
UK & Republic of Ireland 11.00
US & Canada Newfoundland Time 07.30, Atlantic Canada Time
07.00, Eastern Standard Time 06.00, Central Time 05.00, Mountain
Time 04.00, Pacific Time 03.00, Alaska 02.00

ARRIVING
By air

Most visitors will arrive by plane at Brnik Airport, which is 27 km
(17 miles) from the city centre. Other airports are available at
Portorož and Maribor, but these tend only to be used by the smaller,
regional carriers. Though Brnik Airport has all of the usual services,
such as duty-free shopping, a bureaux de change and café, it does
sometimes feel like you're landing in a farmer's field.

A taxi will take approximately 30–45 minutes to reach the city
centre, depending on traffic, and cost in the region of 7,000 SIT.
Frequent bus services provide the most affordable option for airport
transfer. However, this service is drastically reduced on weekends, so
check schedules in advance. By bus, you will reach Ljubljana in about

40 minutes, depending on the number of stops and traffic. The cost of a one-way ticket is between 740 and 1,000 SIT, depending on which company you use. Buses leaves the airport every hour on the

🔺 *Mestni trg's towering Robba Fountain*

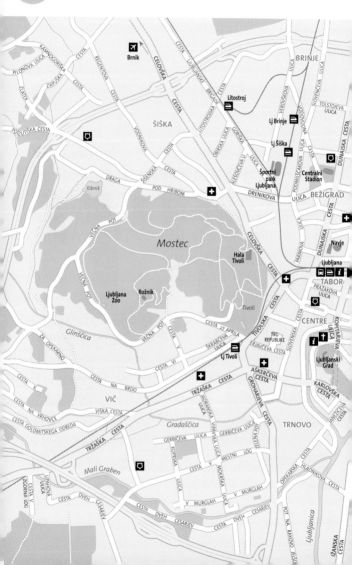

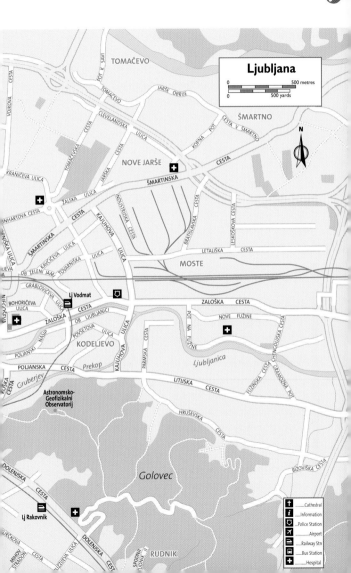

Ljubljana

0 — 500 metres
0 — 500 yards

TOMAČEVO

ŠMARTNO

N

NOVE JARŠE

MOSTE

KODELJEVO

Astronomsko-
Geofizikalni
Observatorij

Golovec

RUDNIK

Lj Vodmat

Lj Rakovnik

ZALOŠKA CESTA

NOVE FUŽINE

Ljubljanica

LITIJSKA CESTA

HRUŠEVSKA CESTA

BIZOVIŠKA CESTA

Gruberjev
Prekop

POLJANSKA CESTA

✝ ......Cathedral
ℹ .....Information
◉ .....Police Station
✈ .....Airport
🚉 .....Railway Stn
🚌 .....Bus Station
✚ .....Hospital

hour from 05.00–20.00 Mon–Fri, or at 07.00 and then every two hours between 10.00 and 20.00 on weekends and holidays. From the city centre, it's the same schedule, but buses leave at ten past the hour instead of on the hour. The journey time is 45 minutes. Markun ☎ 04 252 1016 offers a private bus service between the airport and Ljubljana Bus Station, which departs from the airport daily at 07.30, 09.55, 11.30, 13.45, 15.00, 16.00, 18.10, 21.50, 23.00 and 24.00. Buses for the airport leave Ljubljana at 05.20, 06.15, 10.25, 12.15, 14.10, 15.30, 17.00 and 22.30. The journey time is 30 minutes and the fare is 1,000 SIT.

By rail
Ljubljana doesn't have an extensive rail system, but it can be reached from most parts of Europe. The main line used by locals is

IF YOU GET LOST, TRY ...

Excuse me, do you speak English?
Oprostite, ali govorite angleško?
Oprossteeteh, alee govoreeteh angleshko?

Excuse me, is this the right way to ... the cathedral/the tourist office/the castle/the old town?
Oprostite, je to prava pot do ... Katedrale/turističnega urada/starega mesta?
Oprossteeteh, yeh to prava pot do ... Katedraleh/tooreesteechnega oorada/starega messta?

Can you point to it on my map?
Mi lahko pokažete na karti mesta?
Mee lakhko pokazheteh na kartee messta?

the one that runs between Ljubljana and Maribor, the second-largest city of Slovenia. This line also has spurs that branch off to Novo Mesto and Zagreb (Croatia) via Sevnica. Other lines include a north-south line that runs from the Croatian coast up to the Austrian border via Ljubljana, and another line that avoids the capital altogether, running close to the coast and into Italy.

When in doubt, choose to travel by bus. Not only do the buses run more frequently, they also tend to drop off passengers in more central locations. In some cases, train stations named after a prominent town are actually located many kilometres from your desired destination.

By road
Slovenia is an easy country to drive in, unless you have a fear of heights. Mountainous roads are limited to single lanes and can wind precariously for hours. City streets are well marked and well lit, and the motorway system is fast – except on Friday and Sunday evenings – efficient and extensive. From the cities of Western Europe, drive either to Trieste in Italy, where you can go northeast by picking up the E61/E70/A1 to Ljubljana, or cut down through Germany and Austria and join the E61/A2 southeast to Ljubljana via Bled. From here, it is relatively easy to get into the centre by following the signs. Parking is available both on-street and in protected lots. You may even qualify for free parking at your hotel. Consider selecting a more expensive property that includes parking in the room cost, if you plan on bringing your car.

FINDING YOUR FEET
Ljubljana is a small city of individual neighbourhoods. When exploring specific districts, walking is the best option. However, a

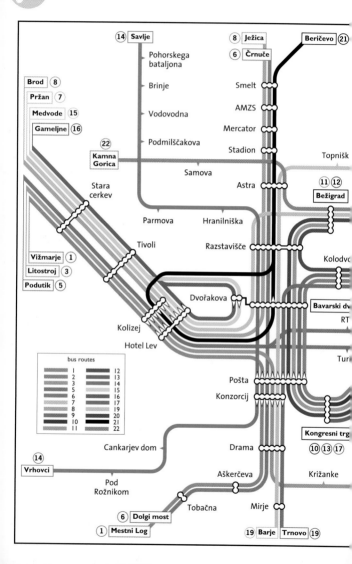

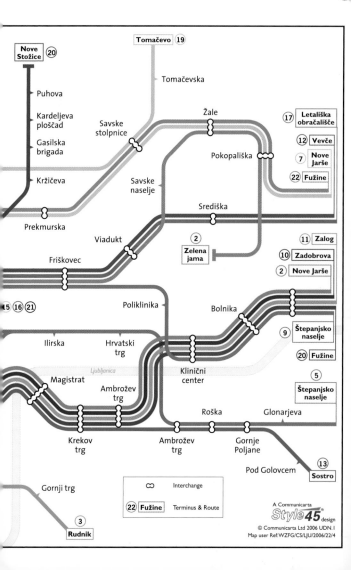

well-maintained network of buses is available. For travel between districts, taxis can be used but they're expensive – and on weekends they're very hard to find.

ORIENTATION

The Slovenian capital is a compact city with the Ljubljanica River cutting right through the centre. The Old Town is situated on the right bank and is made up of short, thin streets that were designed to accommodate little more than horse traffic. This is the neighbourhood that can trace its history back the furthest. As such, roads in this neighbourhood can get quite clogged, due to their modest size.

Ljubljana Castle lies on a hill overlooking this part of town and can be reached using a series of various staircases or winding roads. To save time or energy, board one of the regular trains that depart from Prešeren trg throughout the day.

The Left Bank, opened up following the completion of bridges during the 17th century, offers wider streets and larger properties. Here is where the influence of local architect Jože Plečnik is most strongly felt. The bulk of the city's famed art nouveau masterpieces can also be found here, on Miklošičeva Cesta, running north from Prešeren trg.

As you follow the Left Bank district westwards, it becomes the 'Centre' neighbourhood – a bustling community of government buildings and cultural institutions. While the architecture becomes less interesting in this part of town, the volume of museums grows, especially on the aptly named Muzejska ulica.

Furthest to the west is Tivoli park, a 5 sq km (2 sq mile) swathe of greenery that is well used and well loved by residents. During the day, joggers, cyclists and skateboarders all congregate on the numerous paths, while office workers set up picnics during their lunch hours. Sights in this part of town are few, but the natural beauty more than makes up for the lack of landmarks.

The residential neighbourhoods of Krakovo and Trnovo lie to the south. Visit this region if you want to experience a slice of Slovenian life. Artists, students and bohemians call this district home, and the result is a colourful collection of cafés, street-scenes and nightspots that are well worth an evening or two of your time.

⬤ *Playing on the steps of the School of Music*

GETTING AROUND

Ljubljana is an extremely easy city to get around. While there is a system of buses and trains, you probably won't ever need to use these, as the city centre is so tiny. From Prešeren trg, it's possible to get anywhere in town (including the farthest reaches of Tivoli) in about 15–20 minutes at a brisk walking pace. If you are feeling a little lazy, there are 21 bus routes to choose from, running approximately every 15 minutes from 05.00–22.30. Single journeys can be paid for on-board and cost a flat rate of 300 SIT. If you plan on making several journeys, pick up plastic tokens for 190 SIT at the post office or newsstands. For a map of the bus system, see pages 54–5.

CAR HIRE

Unless you're planning to drive out to Eastern Slovenia or further afield, you won't need to hire a car. While driving isn't a problem, the national bus and rail systems are just too extensive to warrant the expense of car hire. Also, some of the mountainous roads can be quite treacherous, so if you have a fear of heights you may want to avoid driving altogether.

Rates vary according to season and length of hire, but special offers are available – check the internet. The minimum age for renting a car varies between 18 and 21.

● *The Italianete Franciscan Church on the Left Bank*

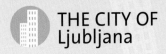
THE CITY OF
Ljubljana

Old Town

Ljubljana's Old Town is the ancient heart of the city. Winding streets, cobbled passages and a stunning hilltop castle provide plenty of atmosphere that is tailor-made for romance and intrigue. For the best views over Ljubljana and beyond, head straight to the top of the Castle Belvedere tower.

The Old Town is where you will find the best shopping, most historic buildings and secret architectural finds. Pick up a few goodies at the Central Market before getting lost in the maze-like streets. Only by wandering the Old Town's courtyards and lanes will you truly be able to savour everything that this ancient neighbourhood has to offer.

SIGHTS & ATTRACTIONS

Botanični Vrt (Botanical Garden)

Situated 800 m (2,625 ft) southeast of Old Town proper, this small collection of flora was founded in 1810 and contains approximately 4,500 species of plants, trees and flowers, of which about one-third are native to Slovenia.

ⓐ Ižanska cesta 15 ⓣ 01 427 1280 ⓛ 07.00–19.00 Apr–Oct, 07.00–17.00 Nov–Mar

Cathedral

It may not have an original name, but Ljubljana's cathedral boasts a long and proud history. A church has existed in this location since the 13th century, but the present structure only harks back to the early 1700s. While the interiors aren't to everyone's taste – all baroque gilt, pink marble, stucco and frescoes – the choir

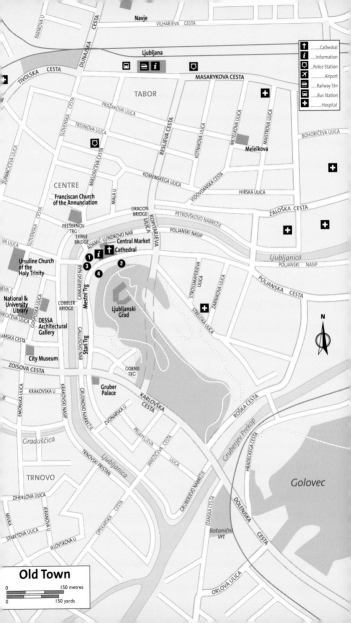

Old Town

✝	......Cathedral
ℹ	......Information
Ⓟ	......Police Station
✈	......Airport
🚉	......Railway Stn
🚌	......Bus Station
✚	......Hospital

Navje
VILHARJEVA CESTA
Ljubljana
MASARYKOVA CESTA
TABOR
DUNAJSKA CESTA
TIVOLSKA CESTA
PARMOVA U
PRAŽAKOVA ULICA
TRDINOVA ULICA
SLOVENSKA CESTA
RESLJEVA CESTA
KOTNIKOVA ULICA
METELKOVA ULICA
MASTNOVA ULICA
Meleikova
BOHORIČEVA ULICA
ŽUPANČIČEVA U
MIKLOŠIČEVA CESTA
KOMENSKEGA ULICA
VIDOVDANSKA CESTA
HIRSKA ULICA
CENTRE
Franciscan Church
of the Annunciation
MALU U
DRAGON
BRIDGE
KOPITARJEVA ULICA
PETKOVŠKOVO NABREŽJE
POLJANSKI NASIP
ZALOŠKA CESTA
PREŠERNOV
TRG
TRIPLE
BRIDGE
ADAMIC-LUNDROVO NAB
Central Market
Cathedral
Ljubljanica
POLJANSKI NASIP
VA ULICA
SLOVENSKA C
Ursuline Church
of the
Holy Trinity
CANKARJEVO NAB
❶ ℹ
❸
❹
❷
STROSSMAYERJEVA ULICA
ZARNIKOVA ULICA
POLJANSKA CESTA
Mestni Trg
National &
University
Library
COBBLER
BRIDGE
Ljubljanski
Grad
STRELIŠKA ULICA
GORNJI
TRG
DESSA
Architectural
Gallery
GOSPOSKA ULICA
KRIŽEVNIŠKA ULICA
GALLUSOVO NAB
Stari Trg
City Museum
ZOISOVA CESTA
KRAKOVSKA U
KRAKOVSKI NASIP
ČEVLJARSKA U
Gruber
Palace
KARLOVŠKA
CESTA
ROŠKA CESTA
EMONSKA ULICA
ZVONARSKA U
PRIJATELJEVA ULICA
Gradaščica
TRNOVSKI PRISTAN
Ljubljanica
JANEŽIČEVA ULICA
GRUBERJEVO NABREŽJE
Gruberjev Prekop
Golovec
TRNOVO
ŽIHERLOVA ULICA
TRŽAŠKA CESTA
MINKA
ŠTARETOVA ULICA
JELOVŠKOVA U
OPEKARSKA CESTA
ZANSKA CESTA
DOLENJSKA CESTA
Botanični
Vrt
ORLOVA ULICA

N

0 ___ 150 metres
0 ___ 150 yards

stalls are spectacular. The two bronze doors at the main entrance are a recent addition, introduced to celebrate the visit of Pope John Paul II in 1996.

ⓐ Dolničarjeva ulica 1 ⓣ 01 231 0684 ⓛ 10.00–12.00 & 15.00–18.00

Cobbler Bridge

Many consider the bridges of Ljubljana to be the most famous sights in the city – and for good reason. Cobbler Bridge, when originally built, was intended as a centre for trade and it created a lot of revenue for the feudal lords through the tolls collected from all who used it to pass in and out of the Old City.

Dragon Bridge

This bridge is the last of the four famous bridges to cross the Ljubljanica, yet is also one of its most graceful. Built in the early 20th century, the bridge is topped by dragons. There is an old legend that says the dragons will wag their tales each time a virgin passes.

Gornji Trg (Gornji Square)

This extension of Stari trg is notable for its collection of medieval houses and the Church of St Florian – a place of worship built in 1672 after a devastating fire that destroyed much of the old town. The church is dedicated to the patron saint of fires.

Mestni Trg (Town Square)

This is the most important square in the Old Town and would have been the focal point of all activity during the Middle Ages. Today the name is given to a more extensive area of side streets. Overlooking proceedings is the town hall, which remains the seat of city government – a role it has performed since it was built in the late

15th century. Inside is a Gothic courtyard with an arcade that once hosted theatrical performances. Unfortunately, this is no longer possible. Lying on top of the building is the symbol of Ljubljana, a golden dragon.

Stari Trg (Old Square)

Stari trg is the traditional heart of the Old Town. Here is where the shops of yesteryear would have battled it out for the wallets of Ljubljana's medieval residents. The houses that line the square today are reconstructions from the 19th century, but a few of the original buildings can be spotted if you take a quick jaunt down the adjoining cobbled passageways and into the serene courtyards.

⬥ *The dragon is a traditional symbol for the city*

Triple Bridge

Leading from Prešernov trg to Old Town, the Triple Bridge is the main span that crosses the Ljubljanica River and also one of the most admired. Designed by the architect Jože Plečnik in 1943, the bridge is essentially a combination of the original Špital Bridge with two (almost) parallel spans to form a... you guessed it... triple bridge. In terms of foot traffic, it remains the most-used bridge in the city.

◓ *Ljubljana's castle dominates the city's skyline*

CULTURE

Gruber Palace

This palace, which now holds the collections of the national archives, was the original home of Gabriel Gruber. A prominent Jesuit, Gruber was responsible for building the canal that regulates the Ljubljanica River. The palace is a rare example of the Zopf style, a transitional architectural style that bridged the gap between late baroque and neoclassicism in the early 18th century.

From the main entrance, look east along the Karlovška cesta where you will see what remains of the city's old Balkan Gate.

🅰 Zvezdarska ulica 1; visit by appointment only, in person

Ljubljanski Grad (Ljubljana Castle)

Ljubljana Castle, built in the 16th century, dominates the skyline as it stands imperiously on the top of Castle Hill. Considered the most important spot in the city, due to its location on top of the region's highest point, the castle was a royal residence through much of the 17th and 18th centuries.

As the castle fell out of favour architecturally, its strong walls and fortifications proved excellent assets for the national barracks and prison until well into the 20th century.

Today, the bulk of the castle has been renovated to its original splendour and most traces of the prison have been erased.

Try to include a visit to the Belvedere. This tower, located on the western side of the castle courtyard, provides stunning views over the entire city and beyond to the Alps. The extra expense is certainly worth the investment. Also of interest is a stop at the Virtual Museum, a 20-minute 3-D movie that takes visitors on a quick tour through Ljubljana's most influential periods.

While climbing up the Belvedere Tower, give yourself a few minutes to peak inside the Chapel of Saint George. Built in 1489, this fresco-covered place of worship features many depictions of the coats of arms of Ljubljana's ruling families.

Guided tours of the castle, museum, tower and grounds are available during the summer months at 10.00 and 16.00. Join the group on the bridge located at the castle's main entrance. Also, if the prospect of climbing up Castle Hill to see Ljubljanski Grad doesn't appeal, take advantage of the convenient tourist train that leaves from Prešernov trg every hour on the hour between 09.00 & 18.00.

ⓐ Ljubljanski Grad ⓦ www.festival-lj.si ⓛ 09.00–22.00 May–Sept; 10.00–21.00 Oct–Apr; Belvedere 09.00–21.00 May–Sept; 10.00–18.00 Oct–Apr

RETAIL THERAPY

Shopping streets & markets

Central Market There is simply no better place to barter and binge than Ljubljana's Central Market. Lying just across the Triple Bridge from Prešernov trg, this open-air marketplace sells fresh fruit, cheeses and souvenirs all week long.

Other seasonal markets worth a look are the arts and crafts market held every Friday morning and the Sunday-morning antique market held in Pogačarjev trg.

Dom Excellent carved wooden objets d'art and locally produced pottery are just some of the speciality items found at this pleasant home furnishings store. ⓐ Mestni trg 24 ⓣ 01 241 8300 ⓛ 09.00–19.00 Mon–Fri, 10.00–15.00 Sat

Rustika For convenience, you can't beat the wares on offer at this souvenir shop and art gallery located inside Ljubljana Castle. Quality is better than average. ⓐ Ljubljanski Grad ⓣ 031 383 247 ⓘ 10.00–19.00 Oct–May, 09.30–20.00 June–Sept

Trigi Store Football shirts and paraphernalia make great gifts for the guys back home. Pick up a few Slovenian football strips at this well-priced sporting goods store. ⓐ Ciril-Meto-dov trg 19 ⓣ 01 430 0191 ⓘ 09.00–19.00 Mon–Fri, until 13.00 Sat

Tubarjev Antikvariat Second-hand and antiquarian books that are good both for novices and seasoned collectors. Many of the titles are printed in Slovenian or other Balkan languages. ⓐ Mestni trg 25

⬥ *A guided tour of the city, on wheels*

☎ 01 244 2683 **⏱** 08.30–13.00 & 17.00–20.00 Mon–Fri, 08.30–13.00 & 16.00–19.00 Sat

TAKING A BREAK

Abecedarium Café £ ❶ Once the residence of a famous Slovenian writer, this house (the oldest in Ljubljana, dating back to 1528) is now a delightful teahouse that serves up coffees, pastries and many more treats. **ⓐ** Ribji trg 2 **☎** 01 426 9514 **⏱** 07.00–13.00 Mon–Sun

AFTER DARK

Restaurants

Sokol £–££ ❷ While the interiors are far from authentic, the food certainly is. Everyone – from little old ladies to market traders – pops in to this faux-rustic eatery to nosh on local nibbles or grab a cup of coffee. **ⓐ** Metodov trg 18 **☎** 01 439 6855 **⏱** 06.30–23.00 Mon–Sat, 12.00–22.00 Sun

Zlata Ribica £–££ ❸ Translated from Slovenian, the name of this restaurant is Goldfish. Ironically, fish is the last thing you will find on the menu. Meat eaters will rejoice at the sight of the heavy traditional Slovenian dishes – including game and pheasant – coming from the kitchen. **ⓐ** Cankarjevo nabrežje 5–7 **☎** 01 426 9490 **⏱** 08.00–23.00 Mon–Sun

Chez Eric ££ ❹ On warm evenings, an outdoor table at this popular French restaurant is like gold dust. The menu changes daily, but you can always guarantee that four fish and four meat dishes will be available to choose from. **ⓐ** Mestni trg 3 **☎** 01 251

2839 🕐 12.00–23.00 Mon–Sat Sept–May; 12.00–24.00 Mon–Sun June–Aug

Bars, clubs & discos

Bar Ljubljanski Grad If you opt out of trying to reach the top of Castle Hill, then this bar provides plenty of options to help you get your breath back. Not worth going out of your way to visit. ⓐ Ljubljanski Grad ⓣ 01 439 4140 🕐 09.00–24.00 May–Sept; 10.00–21.00 Oct–Apr

Bar Minimal This bar is exactly what it says it is – minimal. Decorated in various shades of white, it attracts a hipper-than-thou crowd. Luckily the cocktails and the soulful soundtrack are worth suffering through the snob factor. ⓐ Mestni trg 4 ⓣ 01 426 0138 🕐 08.00–01.00 Mon–Sun

Fraga For those who like a bit of art while they drink, then enjoy an alcoholic bevvie (or two) at this combination art gallery/lounge bar. ⓐ Mestni trg 15 ⓣ 01 426 9005 🕐 09.00–01.00 Mon–Sun

Maček This bar/café situated directly on the right bank of the Ljubljanica is the place to see and be seen. On summer afternoons, a table is almost impossible to get. ⓐ Krojaška ulica 5 ⓣ 01 425 3791 🕐 08.30–00.30 Mon–Sun

Movia Vinoteka Drink your way through the wines of Slovenia at this well-stocked wine bar. Regular wine tastings that highlight local vintages are programmed. If you like the bottle you're sipping, they can even arrange to ship a case to your home. ⓐ Mestni trg 2 ⓣ 01 425 5448 🕐 12.00–24.00 Mon–Fri, 10.00–24.00 Sat

Left Bank Centre

Ljubljana's Left Bank is the place where locals do their business, meet up with friends, are entertained and savour culture. Here is where you'll find the best galleries and museums, the most attractive bars, and the finest examples of art nouveau construction. The Left Bank grew in popularity as the Old Town began to grow outside the ancient city walls. Aristocrats were drawn to the larger plots of land and greater privacy afforded by the neighbourhoods across the river and they moved in droves. Today's chic and elite continue to flock to the Left Bank – this time in search of the perfect riverside table to enjoy drinks and dinner with friends. On summer evenings, the cafés alongside the Ljubljanica River swarm with activity.

SIGHTS & ATTRACTIONS

Franciscan Church of the Annunciation

From the exterior, this church looks like it should have some promising treasures lying within. Unfortunately, with the exception of a glass coffin holding the rather gruesome remains of a saint by the name of Deodatus, there is little to warrant a trip inside this 17th-century Italianate structure.

ⓐ Prešernov trg 4 ❶ 01 425 3007 ● 06.45–12.30 & 15.00–20.00 Mon–Sun

Kongresni Trg (Congress Square)

Ljubljana hosted the Congress of the Holy Alliance between Austria, Russia, Naples and Prussia in 1821 and this is the square named to honour the event. In the centre of the square is a park known as

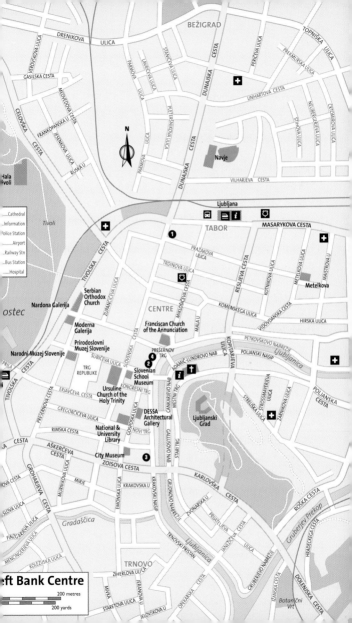

Zvezda (star), due to the shape in which the trees are planted. You may find yourself surrounded by students at all hours of the day, due to the placement of Ljubljana University in a former ducal palace on the square's southern edge.

Miklošičeva Cesta

This main road links Prešernov trg with the train and bus stations, and is considered to have the finest examples of art nouveau construction in town. Buildings to look out for include the Grand Union Hotel, built in 1905 and still thought of as the fanciest hotel in Ljubljana, the People's Loan Bank at No 4, the Cooperative Bank with its colourful geometric patterns at No 8, and the buildings that face Miklošičev Park. Promenading along this stretch of road is a favoured pastime among courting couples and families.

Novi Trg (New Square)

This meeting point south of the Cobbler's Bridge was originally situated outside the city walls in the Middle Ages. Fishermen called the area home until the 16th century when aristocrats, charmed by the houses, decided to move in and gentrify the properties. Though many of the homes were destroyed during an earthquake in 1895, the square continues to be of interest due to the remains of the medieval Jewish quarter on Židovska ulica. The synagogue and much of the Jewish population are now gone, but the area retains a lot of its character. The Slovenian Academy of Arts and Sciences is situated on the square's western end, and occasionally hosts intriguing exhibitions.

▶ *Prešeren, the famous Slovenian poet*

Prešernov Trg (Prešernov Square)

Dedicated to the great Slovenian poet, this central square acts as the main artery linking the Left Bank with the Old Town. Considered the heart of the city, it is often used in summer for free concerts on warm evenings. Note the fine art nouveau architecture in the surrounding streets, and the statue erected in 1905, depicting Prešeren himself. Look closely at the plinth to see depictions and motifs of his most famous poems.

Serbian Orthodox Church

Every inch of this church's wall and ceiling-space is covered with modern frescoes. Dedicated to Saints Cyril and Methodius, it was built in 1936 and remains a popular place of worship for the local Serbian community.

🅐 Prešernova cesta ☎ 01 252 4002 🕓 14.00–18.00 Tues–Sun

Trg Republike (Republic Square)

The district's main square is also its most disappointing. Home to the Slovenian Parliament building, this concrete-strewn example of brutal communist architecture from the late 1950s is an uninspiring mess of tower blocks and exhaust fumes. Go only if you have an interest in Eastern bloc architecture.

Ursuline Church of the Holy Trinity

Probably the most beautiful example of baroque architecture in the city, this church was built in 1726 and contains a spectacular African marble altar of many colours. To reach the church, go along the Plečnik underpass at the western end of Kongresni trg. As you approach the entrance, look to the right to see a golden statue resting at the top of a column. This statue is a copy of the

4th-century *Citizen of Emona*. The original is currently in the National Museum.

🅐 Slovenska cesta 21 🕐 01 252 4864 🕓 09.00–10.30 & 16.30–19.00 Mon–Sun

CULTURE

City Museum

This small museum houses a collection of Roman artefacts that were discovered in and around the city, and a scale model of the ancient city of Emona, upon which Ljubljana now rests.

🅐 Gosposka ulica 15 🕐 01 426 3567 🔍 www.mm-lj.si 🕓 10.00–18.00 Tues–Sun

DESSA Architectural Gallery

This small gallery focuses on the work of the nation's finest contemporary architects.

🅐 Židovska steza 4 🕐 01 251 6010 🕓 10.00–15.00 Mon–Fri

Moderna Galerija (Museum of Modern Art)

This rather unattractive building hosts the works of Slovenia's established contemporary artists and a slew of exciting up-and-comers. Slovenian expressionism, surrealism and socialist-inspired periods are all covered.

🅐 Cankarjeva cesta 15 🕐 01 241 6800 🔍 www.mg-lj.si 🕓 11.00–20.00 Tues–Sun

Narodni Muzej Slovenije (National Museum of Slovenia)

This museum, considered by most to be the finest in the country, boasts a strong coin collection, and sections devoted to applied arts and history. While the Roman artefacts are pretty standard, the Vače situla Celtic pail unearthed east of Ljubljana is a highlight. Displays are being extensively reorganised, so call ahead in order to verify that the collections you want to see aren't off-limits the day you decide to visit.

ⓐ Muzejska ulica 1 ⓣ 01 241 4400 ⓦ www.narmuz-lj.si
ⓛ 10.00–18.00 Fri–Wed, until 20.00 Thur

Narodna Galerija (National Gallery)
For an introduction to Slovenian art, head directly to this extensive gallery of portraits and landscapes. Works include medieval frescoes, Gothic statues, and beautiful pieces from the hands of the national romantics (Künl, Karinger and Pernhart) and impressionists (Šubic and Jakopič). For pieces from outside Slovenia, including items from the Middle Ages and modern day, visit the modern north wing, which also houses temporary exhibitions and visiting artists.

ⓐ Prešernova ulica 24 ⓣ 01 241 5434 ⓦ www.ng-slo.si ⓛ 10.00–18.00 Tues–Sun

National & University Library
Considered to be architect Jože Plečnik's finest work, this building was completed in 1941. The best way to experience the structure is to enter through the main doors and ascend the black marble steps. As you go higher up the staircase, you will emerge into a light-drenched colonnade. According to Plečnik, it is supposed to represent the light of knowledge. The effect is quite inspiring. Continue into the Main Reading Room to see more of the great architect's design work. The lamps are particularly beautiful.

ⓐ Gosposka ulica 14 ⓣ 01 200 1100 ⓛ 09.00–20.00 Mon–Fri, until 13.00 Sat

Prirodoslovni Muzej Slovenije (Slovenian Museum of Natural History)

Sharing the same building as the National Museum, this collection of natural artefacts contains examples of reconstructed mammoth skeletons, stuffed birds, mammals and reptiles. Of particular interest are the mineral exhibits compiled by a 19th-century Baron and a display examining the unique salamander found in the Postojna Caves, *Proteus anguinus* (otherwise known as the 'human fish').

ⓐ Muzejska ulica 1 ⓣ 01 241 0940 ⓛ 10.00–18.00 Mon, Wed, Fri & Sat, until 20.00 Thur, 13.00–18.00 Sun

Slovenian School Museum

Ever wanted to see how Slovenians studied? Teachers may find this small museum of great interest; others may be bored to tears.

ⓐ Plečnikov trg 1 ⓣ 01 251 3024 ⓦ www.sskolski-muzej.si ⓛ 09.00–13.00 Mon–Fri

RETAIL THERAPY

Slovenska is not only a major shopping street, but contains great art nouveau architecture.

Almira Sadar This leading Slovenian designer concocts amazing garments using materials that are 100 per cent natural. ⓐ Tavčarjeva ulica 6 ⓣ 01 430 1329 ⓛ 09.00–19.00 Mon–Fri, until 13.00 Sat

Antikvitete Novak Antiques, both authentic and reproduction. ⓐ Kongresni trg 1 ⓣ 01 426 6541 ⓛ 10.00–13.00 and 16.00–19.00 Mon–Fri, 10.00–13.00 Sat

Vinoteka Simon Bradeško Large wine cellar with a great selection of Slovenian wines. ⓐ Dunajska cesta 18 ⓣ 01 431 5015 ⓛ 10.00–19.00 Mon–Fri, 09.00–13.00 Sat

TAKING A BREAK

Burek stand ❶ If you're about to embark on a bus or train journey and you need a bite before you board, drop by this stand southwest of the station for the best cheese, meat and apple *burek* (filo pastry filled with feta cheese and beef mince) in town. ⓐ Pražakova ulica 2 ⓛ Open 24 hrs, Mon–Sun

AFTER DARK

Restaurants

Cantina Mexicana £–££ ❷ Mexican food in Slovenia? Surprisingly, it works. While the food is good, the location and interiors provide the special touch that makes this place a great local for a leisurely meal. ⓐ Knafljev prehod 3 ⓣ 01 426 9325 ⓐ 09.00–24.00 Mon–Sun

Pri Vitezu ££ ❸ Go to this intimate eatery directly on the left bank of the Ljubljanica for something truly special. Enjoy the Mediterranean and Adriatic fish dishes either in the vaulted wine cellar or adjoining bar. ⓐ Breg 18–20 ⓣ 01 426 6058 ⓛ 12.00–24.00 Mon–Sat

Gostlina As ££–£££ ❹ Delicious seafood tailor-made for special occasions. The wine list is particularly well-chosen. ⓐ Knafljev prehod 5a ⓣ 01 425 8822 ⓛ 12.00–24.00 Mon–Sun

ⓓ *So famous with locals, the* Burek *Stand has no formal name*

Bars, clubs & discos

Bacchus Centre Club This clubbing centre has a restaurant, lounge-bar and large dancefloor, so you're bound to find something you like. Probably the most popular place in town. ⓐ Kongresni trg 3 ⓘ 01 241 8244 ⓒ 22.00–04.00 Wed–Sat

Metelkova Inspired by the squatters of Copenhagen's Christiania, a group of locals took over former army barracks and transformed them into Metelkova. A number of clubs call this location home,

⬥ *A patchwork of architecture on the riverbank*

including a hardcore punk venue (Channel Zero), mainstream centre for international DJs (Klub Gromka) and a gay and lesbian bar. Opening times and venues change frequently. ❸ Between Metelkova ulica & Maistrova ulica ⓦ www.metelkova.org

Papillon Named after the book and subsequent film starring Steve McQueen and Dustin Hoffman, this club is designed to look like a well-heeled prison. Less tacky than it sounds. ❸ Nazorjeva ulica 6 ❶ 01 426 2126 ⏱ 10.00–15.00 Wed–Sat

Cinemas & theatres

Café Teater For modern comedies, musicals and popular entertainment, book tickets at Café Teater, located in the Knights Hall of the Križanke arts complex. ❸ trg Francoske Revolucije 1–2 ❶ 01 252 7108 ⓦ www.cafe-teater.si ⏱ variable

Cankanjev Dom The main venue for concerts and performances is this cultural centre named in honour of the novelist and playwright, Ivan Cankar. Two large auditoriums and a dozen smaller performance spaces designed for acoustic sets and chamber music host over a thousand cultural events each year. Acoustics in the Gallus Hall are said to be superb. ❸ Prešernova cesta 10 ❶ 01 241 7300 ⓦ www.cd-cc.si ⏱ variable

Križanke Home to the Ljubljana Summer Festival, this arts complex has had a long and varied history. The Teutonic Knights of the Cross built this as their command centre in the 13th century and it acted as a focal point for city power until 1714, when it was transformed into a monastery. Today, it houses an open-air theatre with seating for 1,400 people. Look immediately in front of the complex for the Ilirija Column, dedicated to Napoleon. Slovenians greatly admired and respected Napoleon because he made Ljubljana his regional capital and allowed Slovenian to be taught in school for the first time in the country's history. **a** trg Francoske Revolucije 1–2 **t** 01 241 6000 **c** variable

Opera House Built in 1892, and originally named the 'Provincial Theatre', this theatre once programmed a season of German and Slovene productions. Today, it houses the Slovenian National Opera and Ballet companies, and performances are in Slovene only. **a** Župančičeva ulica 1 **t** 01 241 1702 **w** www.operainbalet-lj.si **c** variable

Philharmonic Hall The Slovenian Philharmonic Orchestra was founded in 1701 and is now one of the oldest in the world in continuous operation. Honorary members have included Beethoven, Brahms and Haydn, while Gustav Mahler was resident conductor during the season of 1881–82. **a** Kongreni trg 10 **t** 01 241 0800 **c** variable

Slovenian National Drama Theatre Built in 1911, this lovely slice of art nouveau now houses Slovenia's national theatre company. Performances are in Slovenian only. **a** Erjavčeva cesta 1 **t** 01 252 1462 **c** variable

◗ *Look carefully for the detail carved on state buildings*

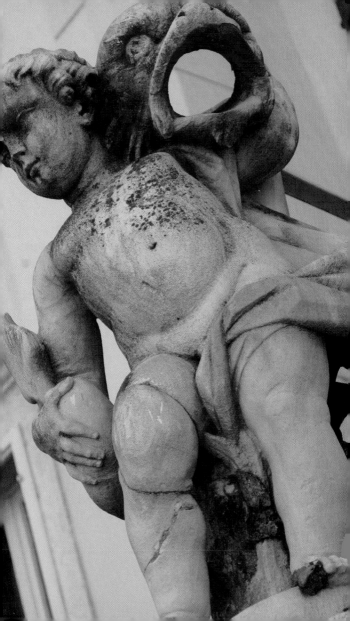

Krakovo & Trnovo

The two neighbourhoods of Krakovo and Trnovo are often ignored by tourists who usually favour the more obvious sights of the city centre. To do this is to miss Ljubljana's residential heart. These two districts, located to the south of the Old Town, offer a number of interesting buildings – many built by the area's local hero, architect Jože Plečnik.

Once considered Ljubljana's Montmartre, due to the number of artists who called its streets home, Krakovo and Trnovo still have a strong artistic flavour. To experience 'La Vie Boheme', head down to the bars along the Ljubljanica near the Trnovo Bridge. The people-watching possibilities in warm weather are top-notch.

SIGHTS & ATTRACTIONS

Church of St John the Baptist

Originally built in 1855, this church is neo-Romanesque in design, yet remains extremely bare inside. With the exception of the ceiling frescoes by artist Matej Sternen, there is very little to warrant a stop. Fans of the work of Prešeren should note that it was inside this church that the poet first saw the love of his life, Julija Primic. Unfortunately for him, she never returned his passions.

ⓐ Kolezijska ulica 1 ❶ 01 283 5060 ❷ 18.00–20.00 Mon–Sat, 08.00–12.00 Sun

Jakopič Garden

Famed Slovenian impressionist Rihard Jakopič worked extensively in this 'garden'. Also the site of some Roman ruins, it is still possible to see the black and white mosaics and remains of a complex heating

Krakovo & Trnovo

0	150 metres
0	150 yards

Cathedral
Information
Police Station
Airport
Railway Stn
Bus Station
Hospital

Golovec

HRADECKEGA CESTA

Grubarjev Prekop

STRELIŠKA ULICA

ROŠKA CESTA

HRADECKEGA CESTA

DOLENJSKA CESTA

DOLENISKA CESTA

ORLOVA ULICA

MENJOVA ULICA

MRZELOVA ULICA

OB DOLENJSKI ŽELEZNICI

Botanic
Gardens

IŽANSKA CESTA

GRUBERJEVO NABREŽJE

PRIVOZ

ULICA

JANEŽIČEVA CESTA

KARLOVŠKA CESTA

PRIJATELJEVA CESTA

ZNAMANSKA U

GORNJI
TRG

Gruber
Palace

STARI TRG

GALLUSOVO NAB

GRUDNOVO NABREŽJE

TRNOVSKI PRISTAN

Ljubljanica

Ljubljanica

VELIKA KOLNIŠKA ULICA

OPEKARSKA CESTA

OPEKARSKA CESTA

HLADNIKOVA CEST

CESTA

TRNOVO
BRIDGE

KRAKOVSKI NASIP

KRAKOVSKA U

KRAKOVO

GRADAŠKA ULICA

EIPPROVA ULICA

JERANOVA U

ŽIHERLOVA ULICA

KOLEZIJSKA ULICA

MIVKA

MIVKA

TRNOVO

CESTA

City Museum

ZOISOVA CESTA

EMONSKA ULICA

& Library

RIMSKA CESTA

GOSPOSKA

Jakopič
Garden

MIRJE

Church of
St John the
Baptist

Plečnik
House &
Collection

MIVKA

STARETOVA ULICA

CESTA NA LOKO

AŠKERČEVA CESTA

BARJANSKA CESTA

Gradaščica

BARSANSKA CESTA

Roman
Wall

MIRJE

MURNIKOVA ULICA

RIHARJEVA ULICA

MENCINGERJEVA ULICA

FINŽGARJEVA ULICA

TESLOVA U

KOLEZIJSKA ULICA

DEVINSKA ULICA

CESTA V MESTNI LOG

V MURGLAH

POD HRASTI

GROHARJEVA CESTA

JANOVA CESTA

ISSA CESTA

ZELENA POT

KOŠESKEGA ULICA

ZBAŠNIKOVA ULICA

CVETLIČNA POT

JAMBROVA

POD TOPO

system. Unless you make plans in advance, it is only possible to view the artefacts from the gate – so if Roman history is of great interest to you, make an appointment before you arrive.

🇦 Mirje 4 ☎ 01 251 4025 🕑 by appointment only

Roman wall

Plečnik came up with the idea of reconstructing the original Roman wall that once circled the city. The result is this stretch, which runs along the length of Mirje. It doesn't quite work, but it's an interesting concept nonetheless.

Trnovo Bridge

Plečnik designed and built this bridge in 1932. Considered one of the three great bridges of Ljubljana (along with the Triple Bridge and Dragon Bridge), this is the one few tourists see due to its distance from the city centre. What makes this bridge so notable is its collection of five pyramids – a Plečnik trademark – that lie alongside it.

CULTURE

Plečnik House & Collection (Ljubljana Architectural Museum)

Plečnik lived in this home from 1921 until his death in 1957. Considered one of Slovenia's finest architects, Plečnik was responsible for the bulk of the city's most highly regarded buildings and bridges. This collection perfectly preserves his books, equipment, furniture and notes almost exactly as they were found at the time of his death. One of the quirkier items is a chair in the

▶ *The original Roman wall that used to surround the city*

kitchen that was specially designed to allow Plečnik to eat and work at the same time.

ⓐ Karunova ulica 4 🕐 10.00–14.00 Tues & Thur

RETAIL THERAPY

While Krakovo and Trnovo may be residential districts, they aren't all that popular when it comes to shopping. Due to Ljubljana's compact size, residents still prefer to make the short trek into the old town to spend their money. As such, the options aren't exactly overwhelming. Convenience stores, supermarkets and uninspiring clothing tend to constitute the bulk of what's on offer. Keep your wallet in your pocket and save your cash for the boutiques in the city centre.

Annapurna Shop If you're considering a trek into the Julian Alps but have forgotton your sleeping bag, then kit yourself out here. Almost anything you might need for all-season explorations is available.
ⓐ Krakovski nasip 4 ☎ 01 426 3428 🕐 09.00–19.00 Mon–Fri, until 13.00 Sat

TAKING A BREAK

For a delightful rest after a day exploring the neighbourhood, look for Eipprova ulica – a leafy street that runs east from the Trnovo Bridge along the southern embankment of Gradaščica. This collection of cafés and bars is colourful and quirky, appealing to the district's artistic and outspoken residents. Choose any of the eateries for a good meal surrounded by friendly local folk. One of the better options is:

Sax Pub £ ❶   Don't be put off by the graffiti. This pub is a great place for a pint and a platter of Slovenian nibbles. Live jazz is offered every Thursday evening at 22.00. ⓐ Eipprova ulica 7 ❶ 01 283 9009 🕒 10.00–01.00 Tues–Sun

🔺 *The marina is a great place to relax*

AFTER DARK

Restaurants

Pri Škofju £ ❷ Especially popular for weekend breakfasts, this tasty restaurant in the heart of Krakovo is considered by many to offer the best Slovenian dishes in town. ⓐ Ręna ulica 8 ❶ 01 426 4508 ⓒ 08.00–24.00 Mon–Fri, 12.00–24.00 Sat & Sun

Pri Jerneju £–££ ❸ Cosy and comfortable *gostilne* (inn) serving solid takes on Slovenian favourites. Definitely one of the better options if you're looking to try local cuisine. ⓐ Velika Čolnarska ulica 17 ❶ 01 283 8735 ⓒ 12.00–23.00 Mon–Sat, until 19.00 Sun

Tera Rósa £–££ ❹ *Wallpaper** magazine raves about Ljubljana, and this restaurant feels like it could have stepped right out of its pages. Sleek and stylish, it's a nice change of pace from the city's homier inns and taverns. Service is spotless, and the dishes of Mediterranean and karst specialities are sure to satisfy. ⓐ Hrenova ulica 19 ❶ 01 425 8824 ⓒ 12.00–23.00 Mon–Sat

Yildiz Han ££ ❺ It can sometimes feel a bit kitsch with all the belly dancing and live Turkish music, but if you're with a group then this Turkish eatery is a lot of fun. Run by a friendly family, it's a solid choice for a spicy, yet tasty, night on the town. ⓐ Karlovška cesta 19 ❶ 01 426 5717 ⓒ 12.00–24.00 Tues–Sun

Bars, clubs & discos

Trnovski Zvon Pub When the Sax is packed, this studenty pub makes for a great second-choice venue. While it's not as hip, it's also not as crowded. Try to sit at one of the outdoor tables to enjoy the street traffic. ⓐ Eipprova ulica 17 ⓣ 01 283 9496 ⓛ 09.00–23.00 Mon–Fri, 11.00–23.00 Sat, 12.00–22.00 Sun

Cinemas & theatres

KUD France Prešeren Centre Dedicated to presenting 'non-traditional' artistic events, this society programmes an eclectic mix of literary events, spoken-word performances, workshops and exhibitions. Not for fans of Broadway musicals. ⓐ Karunova ulica 14 ⓣ 01 283 2288 ⓦ www.kud-fp.si ⓛ 11.00–01.00 Mon–Sun

⬥ *Residential areas are filled with character*

Tivoli

Tivoli draws its name from the massive park situated at its centre. Considered the green lungs of the city, this 5 sq km (2 sq mile) area of parkland, which was designed in 1813, positively heaves on summer days, when locals who haven't got the time or money to head out to the coast or up into the mountains choose to while away their time on the area's grassy slopes. What makes this park special is the fact that this collection of paths, trees and meadows is probably loved more by its residents than New Yorkers love Central Park or Londoners love Hyde Park. Nature is adored by Slovenians – almost all of whom wish that they could afford a country retreat for those weekends when Ljubljana is packed with tourists. As soon as the sun comes out, locals will plan picnics and impromptu kick-about sessions of footie. If you want to join the active crowds, why not consider renting a bicycle at any of the numerous booths?

Whatever you do, don't litter or leave anything behind. Even stubbing out a cigarette is frowned upon. Mother nature deserves respect and the locals won't be afraid to tell you this if they see you doing something that might harm her.

SIGHTS & ATTRACTIONS

Krajinski Park Tivoli

This main green artery of Ljubljana is loved by this city of rural worshippers. It's a popular spot for walking, biking, picnics and outdoor sports. On the southeastern edge of the park is Krajinski Park Tivoli – a series of walkways, fountains and benches that meander through the landscaped grasses. Children especially love the lower level of this orderly park, drawn by the playground and

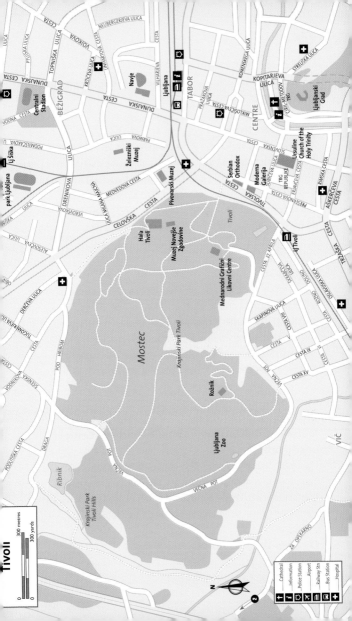

Tivoli

0   300 metres
0   300 yards

N

BEŽIGRAD

Centralni Stadion

Navje

Ljubljana

TABOR

Ljubljanski Grad

CENTRE

park Ljubljana

Železniški Muzej

lj Šiška

Pivovarski Muzej

Serbian Orthodox

Moderna Galerija

Ursuline Church of the Holy Trinity

TRG REPUBLIKE

Hala Tivoli

Muzej Novejše Zgodovine

Tivoli

lj Tivoli

Mednarodni Grafični Likovni Centre

Mostec

Krajinski Park Tivoli

Rožnik

Ribnik

Krajinski Park Tivoli Hills

Ljubljana Zoo

VEČNA POT

VIČ

Cathedral
Information
Police Station
Airport
Railway Stn
Bus Station
Hospital

recreation centre complete with swimming pool, bowling alleys and tennis courts.

Krajinski Park Tivoli Hills

The bulk of the Park Tivoli is made up by a series of hills, of which Rožnik Hill is the most visited. Here is where travellers can find the church of St Mary and a number of countryside restaurants that feel like they should be situated in Bled, rather than minutes from the centre of Ljubljana. Adventurers especially love this section of the park, and can often be found walking, jogging or cycling along the paths.

Ljubljana Zoo

Over 500 animals representing 120 species are on display at this collection located on the southern slope of Rožnik Hill. The cages are a bit small and some of the visitors taunt the animals mercilessly – but children especially love the petting zoo.

ⓐ Živalski Vrt Ljubljana ⓣ 01 244 2188 ⓦ www.zoo-ljubljana.si
ⓛ June–Aug: 09.00–19.00 Tues–Sun; Sept–May: 09.00–16.00 Tues–Sun

CULTURE

Mednarodni Grafični Likovni Centre (International Centre of Graphic Arts)

Housed in the 17th-century Tivoli mansion, this centre hosts the biannual International Biennial of Graphic Arts during odd-numbered years. When not in use for this exposition, temporary exhibitions are offered, changing every three months.

ⓞ *A trip to Ljubljana Zoo is a favourite with the kids*

🅐 Pod turnom 3 ☎ 01 241 3818 🌐 www.mglc-lj.si 🕐 11.00–18.00
Wed–Sun

Muzej Novejše Zgodovine (Museum of Modern History)

Explore the history of Slovenia's last hundred years at this
multimedia-heavy collection of exhibits chronicling the 20th
century. Housed in an 18th-century mansion, the museum examines
both the Communist era and the explosion of commercialism
following the destruction of the Iron Curtain.

🅐 Celovška cesta 23 ☎ 01 300 9610 🌐 www.muzej-nz.si
🕐 10.00–18.00 Tues–Sun

Pivovarski Muzej (Brewery Museum)

Slovenia's favourite beer is Union, and this museum allows you to
wander around the brewery to examine the magic of hops and
yeast. Tours are only available to groups, but individuals can
sometimes get inside if they call ahead to arrange a special visit.
Unless you're really fascinated by beer, don't go out of your way
to book.

🅐 Pivovarniska 2 ☎ 01 471 7340 🕐 08.00–13.00 on first Tues of each
month, by appointment only

Železniški Muzej (Railway Museum)

This museum, spread over two sites, hosts a surprisingly large
collection of locomotives from Slovenia's rail history. Everything
from hulking engines to old-fashioned wagons is on offer, including
items that date back to the early days of the country's network
when the original rails were laid by the Austro-Hungarians.

▶ *A show of strength: monument for the people*

KDOR MIMO GREŠ
NE TOŽI NISEM MRTEV
VUSEM KAR ŽIVIŠ
KAR PROST ZDAJ SMEŠ
ZA ROD GRADIŠ
EM JAZ JE MOJA ŽRTEV

Parmova 35 and Kurilniška 3 📞 01 291 2641 🕐 10.00–13.00
Mon–Thur

AFTER DARK

Restaurants

Casa del Papa £–££ **❶** Dedicated to the memory of Ernest
Hemingway, this restaurant serves up the dishes of the countries
that most influenced him throughout his life: Spain, Cuba and
America. Always popular, it's a great place if another meal of
dumplings and meat just won't do. 📍 Celovška cesta 54a
📞 01 434 3158 🕐 12.00–01.00 Mon–Sun

Pod Rožnikom ££ **❷** Out of the way but well-loved by locals, this
restaurant serves spicy Southern Slavic cuisine, including such
mouth-watering items as *pljeskavica* (spicy meat patties) and
prebranac (beans and onions slow-cooked in an earthernware
pot). Veggie items are few and far between. Go only if you have a
completely empty stomach, as portions can be huge.
📍 Cesta na Rožnik 18 📞 01 251 3446 🕐 10.00–23.00 Mon–Fri,
11.00–23.00 Sat & Sun

Bars, clubs & discos

Cuban Room This Latin dance club is a great place for sizzling salsa
sounds and tantalising tangos. Located just below the Casa del Papa
restaurant. 📍 Celovška cesta 54a 📞 01 434 3158 🕐 18.00–05.00
Mon–Sun

🔘 *You can enjoy a balmy ambience at a riverfront eatery*

Key West Bar Another venue that makes up part of the Casa del Papa entertainment complex, the Key West Bar is a cigar bar and subdued rum cocktail lounge for high-fliers and high-class locals.
ⓐ Celovška cesta 54a ⓣ 01 434 3158 ⓛ 21.00–05.00 Mon–Sun

Sub Sub Club Founded by a collection of local DJs, nights vary wildly according to who happens to spin that evening. However, a crowd of the artistic, challenging and downright scary is guaranteed. Leave flashy duds and full wallets at home if you want to blend in.
ⓐ Celovška cesta 25 ⓣ 01 515 3575 ⓛ 10.00–05.00 Fri & Sat

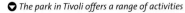

🔽 *The park in Tivoli offers a range of activities*

🔽 *View of boats in the marina*

OUT OF TOWN
trips

Northwest Slovenia

BLED

With the exception of Ljubljana, the town of Bled probably receives more foreign visitors than any other in Slovenia. Tour operators have transformed this pocket of the country into a popular weekend break and outdoor-orientated getaway destination, drawn by its picturesque castle and proximity to the wonders and sporting opportunities of the Julian Alps.

Located on the banks of Lake Bled, the town can get extremely crowded during the summer season, when almost the entire population of Ljubljana flocks to its cooler climbs to escape the heat of the capital. Surrounded by soaring peaks, and offering views of the emerald-hued lake, church-dotted island and cliffside castle, the town offers many reasons to warrant a visit. Medieval pilgrims knew about the beauty of Bled for many years and transformed the area into a place of peace and prayer, most choosing to worship at the Church of the Assumption located on Bled Island in the middle of the lake.

SIGHTS & ATTRACTIONS

Bled Castle

Perched on the top of a rugged cliff, Bled castle looks out over the lake and includes all the features most people associate with a typical medieval fort. Towers, moats, ramparts, ivy-covered walls, atmospheric cellars – all combine to create the perfect setting.

Built on two levels, the castle dates back to the 11th century, but most of what can be seen today was built in the 16th century. The southern wing houses a museum collection including coinage,

Around Ljubljana

0 — 30 km

0 — 15 miles

N

Legend
- City
- Large Town
- Small Town
- Motorway
- Main Road
- Minor Road
- Airport
- Railway

Ljubljana Region

CROATIA

AUSTRIA

ITALY

SLOVENIA

Ptuj

3

Maribor

A9

Maribor ✈

Slov Bistrica

A10

69

3

Sloveni Gradec

4

Velenje

Celje

Javornik ▲ 1023

10-3

Trbovlje

A1

Novo Mesto

Metlika

Kočevje

Kamnik

Ljubljana

H3

A1

Grosuplje

6

Snežnik ▲ 1796

Brnik ✈

1

Kranj

Škofja Loka

Vrhnika

Postojna

10-4

A10

Idrija

Ajdovščina

10-5

A10

12

Novo Gorica

Potorož

12

Trieste

Bled

Ratitovec ▲ 1678

Bohinjska Bištrica

Tolmin

Bovec

Škrlatica ▲ 2738

Triglavski National Park

A23

Udine

A11

Villach

A2

Klagenfurt

A2

80

A23

11

armour, furniture and costume from various periods throughout the region's history. While many of the items were never actually used by the residents of the castle, they serve to give a good insight into how the Slovenian upper classes lived.

There is even an old-fashioned printing press where you can pick up prints of Bled lake scenes and a wine cellar staffed by a monk, selling bottles of local vintages.

ⓐ Grajska cesta 25 ⓣ 04 574 1230 ⓛ 08.00–20.00 May–Oct, 08.00–17.00 Nov–Apr

Bled Island

Site of a Christian church since the 9th century, this jewel of an island is a popular trip. Getting to the island is almost as much fun as exploring the island itself. Trips are made on regular gondolas that depart from Spa Park, the jetty below the Tourist Information Centre and Milno on the south shore. If you're feeling active, you can also rent rowing boats. The main sight on the island is the baroque Church of the Assumption, which can be reached by following the South Staircase (built in 1655) past the Chaplain's House and Provost's House. Outside the church is a 15th-century belfry and wishing bell, which visitors ring if they want to ask for something special.

ⓛ 08.00–dusk

TAKING A BREAK

Slaščičarna Šmon £ Bled has a local pastry speciality in the form of the cream cake – essentially, it's a layer of vanilla custard combined with whipped cream and encased in two layers of flaky pastry. Very

🅞 *The enchanting island in Lake Bled*

sweet. Very rich. And oh, so good. Give a slice a try at this café.
🄰 Grajska cesta 3 🕔 04 574 1616 🕔 variable

AFTER DARK

Restaurants

Gostlina Pletna £ Head to this cheap and cheerful eatery and
pizzeria with an obligatory wood-fired oven. 🄰 Cesta Svobode 37
🕔 04 574 3702 🕔 variable

Mayer Penzion £–££ This Slovenian restaurant puts the focus on
authenticity and uses only the finest local ingredients. Especially
highly regarded for its selection of delicious Slovenian wines.
🄰 Želeška cesta 7 🕔 04 576 5740 🔘 www.mayer-sp.si 🕔 variable

Restavracija Okarina ££ This restaurant is probably the fanciest in
town and dishes up traditional Slovenian options in a romantic
setting. The interior may feel slightly kitsch, though. If it proves too
much, try snaring a table on the back terrace. On weekends, the
restaurant opens up its tandoori oven to add Indian meals to the
menu. 🄰 R|iklijeva cesta 9 🕔 04 574 1458 🕔 variable

Bars, clubs & discos

Casino Bled Casino Bled is the hottest nightspot in town. Roulette,
baccarat, blackjack and slots are all on offer. 🄰 Cesta Svoboda 15
🕔 04 574 1811 🕔 24 hours Mon–Sun

Pub Bled Enjoy drinking and dancing to the wee hours in this
friendly spot located opposite the Grand Hotel Toplice. 🄰 Cesta
Svobode 19a 🕔 04 574 2622

ACCOMMODATION

Penzion Bledec £ This Hostelling International-affiliated hostel offers dorm-style accommodation just steps away from the castle. An affordable restaurant and bar draw a lively crowd of students and young travellers. ⓐ Grajska cesta 17 ⓣ 04 574 5250 ⓦ www.mlino.si

Grand Hotel Toplice ££–£££ Considered one of the finest hotels in the region, it can sometimes feel overrun by tour groups. Look past this, however, to experience a grande dame hotel that dates back to the mid-19th century. Although some of the rooms can feel a tad gloomy, the views of the lake are superb. ⓐ Cesta Svobode 12 ⓣ 04 579 1000 ⓦ www.hotel-toplice.com

Vila Bled £££ This is an exclusive enclave of 30 rooms surrounded by a large park. On-site amenities include a private beach, boat dock and tennis courts. This is the place to book if you have the cash. ⓐ Cesta Svobode 26 ⓣ 04 579 1500 ⓦ www.vila-bled.com

BOHINJ

Bohinj is the name given to the towns, villages, valleys and mountains that make up the region encompassing the Sava Bohinjka basin, southwest of Bled. At the heart of this location is Lake Bohinj, a body of water with strong magical connections to Slovenian folklore.

SIGHTS & ATTRACTIONS

Church of Saint John the Baptist

This small, medieval church is a real find. Filled with frescoes and located at the end of a stone bridge on a reflective lake, the church

is a place of peace and beauty – perfect for a spot of quiet contemplation.

While the nave of the church is Romanesque, the presbytery is Gothic, dating from the mid-15th century. The most spectacular sections of the church are the presbytery's walls, arches and ceiling, which are covered with frescoes depicting biblical scenes. An interesting image to note is the picture of the three men singing above the angels with vampire teeth on the lower walls of the presbytery. These men have goitres, once a common problem for locals, due to the lack of iodine in their diet.

ⓐ Northern side of the Sava Bohinjka ⓒ 09.00–12.00 & 15.00–18.00 June–Sept, Oct–May by appointment only, approach in person

Savica Waterfall

This waterfall is a popular hiking destination, which provides beautiful backdrops as it carves into a gorge 60 m (197 ft) below. As the source of Slovenia's longest river, it's a well-known landmark, located along a well-marked footpath just 4 km (2.5 miles) from the Hotel Zlatorog in Ukanc. The falls are most inspiring just after a heavy rain. During such weather you will need to wear waterproof clothing in order to avoid getting soaked by the spray.

CULTURE

Alpine Dairy Museum

This small collection located in Stara Fužina (about 1.5 km/1 mile north of Ribčev Laz) chronicles the history of dairy farming in the Bohinj valley. Until the late 1950s, this region of Slovenia was the most important producer of dairy foods in the nation, all by traditional methods. Displays in the museum include a mock-up of a

19th-century herder's cottage, old-fashioned presses and vats, and old photographs.

ⓐ Stara Fužina 181 ☎ 04 572 3095 🕐 10.00–12.00 & 16.00–18.00 Tues–Sun Jan–June, Sept & Oct; 11.00–19.00 Tues–Sun July & Aug

Tomaž Godec Museum

Located in Bohinjska Bistrica, the main settlement of the Bohinj region, this museum chronicles the contributions of one of Slovenia's most noted communists. Godec was one of the founding members of the Slovene National Liberation Movement before being captured by the Germans during World War II. His life as a

🔺 *Striking decoration on a house in Bled*

leather tanner, champion skier and mountaineer is examined in the exhibits on display.

ⓐ Zoisova 15 🕐 10.00–12.00 & 16.00–18.00 Tues–Sun May–Oct, 10.00–12.00 & 16.00–18.00 Wed, Sat & Sun Jan–Apr

AFTER DARK

Restaurants

Gostlina Mihovc £ Popular with locals and visitors, this welcoming eatery dishes up thick soups, stews and goulash. Try not to get too drunk on the home-made brandy. ⓐ Stara Fužina 118 🕐 10.00–24.00 variable

Pizzerija Centre £ Toppings are pretty standard (no funky combinations here) but the central location makes up for the limited selection. As the only place to grab a bite in the centre of Ribčev Laz, it can get crowded in season. ⓐ Ribčev Laz ☎ 04 572 3170 🕐 variable

Gostišče Rupa £–££ You'll need a car to reach this delightful tavern located a village over from Studor. Dishes are of the home-cooked variety, featuring spectacularly fresh Bohinj trout, and dumplings made from buckwheat and cheese. Don't go if you aren't hungry. ⓐ Srednja Vas 87 ☎ 04 572 3401 🕐 10.00–24.00 Mon–Sun July & Aug, 10.00–24.00 Tues–Sun Sept–June

ACCOMMODATION

Planšar £ In such a rural location, why not stay in a farmhouse? This friendly place to rest your head is famous for its cheeses and has a comfortable apartment on-site, which can accommodate groups of up to seven people. ⓐ Stara Fužina 179 ❶ 04 572 3095

Penzion Stare £–££ If you want to experience nature without having to trek into the mountains, this property is the one to book. This small pension, north of the Hotel Zlatorog on the Sava Bohinjka River, boasts just nine rooms. Slightly isolated, it can sometimes feel a little removed from the action, but is a perfect place for total peace and relaxation. Few amenities are on offer – just a basic, clean room in a tranquil setting. Discounts are available to youth and student cardholders. ⓐ Ukanc 128 ❶ 04 574 6400

Hotel Jezero ££ This lakeside property is the most central one in the region, situated just steps away from the Tourist Information Centre and the lake. Amenities include an indoor swimming pool, fitness centre and two saunas. During World War II, the Gestapo took over the property as they considered it to be the nicest home in the area. ⓐ Ribčev Laz 51 ❶ 04 572 3375

◓ *The river winds its way through the city streets*

Soča Valley & Istrian Coast

BOVEC

Just 16 km (10 miles) away from the Italian border is this popular natural resort town considered to be the unofficial capital of the Soča Valley. Alpine enthusiasts adore the place, attracted by the wealth of sporting options, soaring mountains and crystal-clear lakes. The ski resort at Kamin is well-equipped and extensive, offering plenty of trails and runs to pack an extended stay. For a truly memorable experience, book a guided trip with one of the former goatherds into the surrounding hills. Tours can be arranged through the Tourist Information Office in the centre of town.

Four buses a day departing every two hours (or so) depart from Ljubljana bus station. Depending on the road conditions, the journey can take anything from two to three hours. Drivers should follow the E61 motorway as far as Kranjska Gora and follow the signs to Borec. Be warned that, once off the motorway, the drive is filled with cliffside twists and turns. Nervous drivers and those afraid of heights need not apply.

SIGHTS & ATTRACTIONS

Hiking & cycling

There are a number of stunning walks and hikes through the surrounding areas, with maps and guided trips available through the local tourist office. The most popular journey takes visitors to the Boka Waterfall, located 5.5 km (3.5 miles) to the southwest of town. For details and prices, contact the tourist office.

ⓐ trg Golobarskih Žrtev 8 ⓣ 05 384 1919

Skiing

The mountains northeast of Bovec hold the Kamin ski centre, a high-altitude alpine centre with a long ski season that sometimes lasts into early May. Fifteen km (9 miles) of pistes and cross-country runs are on offer, served by chairs and T-bars. For non-athletes, a cable car runs all year, offering views of the valley below. For more information or to purchase ski passes at Kamin:

☎ 05 389 6310 🕸 www.bovec.si

Rafting & canoeing

From April to October it is possible to rent a canoe or organise a rafting trip along the Soča River. Rafting trips can be organised on the day and usually take anywhere from two to eight people on a

⬥ *White-water rafting down the Soča River*

10 km (6 mile) journey. Outfitters will include use of a life jacket, windbreaker, long johns, a paddle and helmet in the cost of the trip. Be sure to bring a swimsuit, T-shirt and a towel, as you are sure to get soaked. Kayak and canoe trips are usually done alone, with rentals on an hourly basis. No office or centre, just wander around.

TAKING A BREAK

Gostišče Stari Kovač Every Slovenian town has its pizzeria. This is the local choice for Bovec. ⓐ Rupa 3 ⓣ 05 388 6699 ⓦ www.starikovac.com ⓛ variable

AFTER DARK

Restaurants

Letni Vrt £ This casual eatery serves up grilled meats, fresh trout and, of course, pizza. Located across from the Alp Hotel, it's a nice place for a meal – especially during the summer months when the garden opens up to diners. ⓐ trg Golobarskih Žrtev 12 ⓣ 05 389 6384 ⓛ variable

Martinov Hram £–££ Seafood and grilled meats are the speciality of this centrally located inn. ⓐ trg Golobarskih Žrtev 28 ⓣ 05 388 6214 ⓛ variable

Vančar £–££ This restaurant caters to locals and serves up some of the largest dishes you are ever likely to see. Portions of the regional specialities are massive and heavy on the arteries. As it's located 3 km (2 miles) south of town, you will need private transport. ⓣ 05 389 6076, call for directions ⓛ variable

Bars, clubs & discos
Pink Panter Bar For a late-night drink in Bovec, there aren't a lot of options. This pub is one of the best, despite the slightly odd name.
ⓐ Kaninska Vas 7 ① 031 588 854 ⓒ variable

ACCOMMODATION

Alp Hotel £–££ Centrally located property that's clean, comfortable and offers truly scrumptious beds. Not as pretty as other hotels but does the trick. ⓐ trg Golobarskih Žrtev 48
① 05 388 6040

Pristava Lepena £–££ Cute holiday village set in an idyllic alpine meadow setting. While the complex is located 15 km (9.3 miles) southeast of town, it's perfect for those looking to immerse themselves in nature, rather than in town life. Rooms are located in six traditional houses divided into quaint apartments. ⓐ Lepena 2
① 05 388 9900 ⓦ www.levant.si

Hotel Kanin ££ Standard rooms are made up for by the swimming pool and sauna. Rates are dependent on season and whether you request a balcony. ⓐ Ledina 9 ① 05 388 6021

IDRIJA

Idrija is a picture-perfect locale nestled in a deep basin at the confluence of two rivers. Surrounded by green hills, it's renowned for its natural vistas and was once one of the richest towns in Slovenia, due to its once booming lace-making and mercury mining operations. In fact, 13 per cent of the world's mercury supply originated here during Idrija's peak. Idrija isn't the

place to visit if your idea of a good time is pubs and parties. For a truly local experience, try and plan your trip to coincide with the annual lace-making festival in August. Hourly buses arrive in Ljubljana throughout the day with journeys taking approximately 1½ hours. Please note that the town is not located on any train lines. Drivers should also note that the town isn't accessible using the country's motorway system. The easiest option is to take the E61/70 motorway as far as Predama Castle, turn north on the secondary road and follow the signs.

SIGHTS & ATTRACTIONS

Anthony Mine Shaft

Live out your mining fantasies on this 1¼-hour-long tour that allows you to experience what it was like to be a mercury miner during the town's heyday. The tour begins in an 18th-century call room where miners were assigned each morning to their daily duties. Here, you will watch an interesting 20-minute movie in English that describes the history of both the town and the mine that made it famous.

You will then have to put on heavy coats and helmets with attached torches before entering the shaft into the first mine, which was sunk in the year 1500.

The tour takes a circular journey, during which you will see examples of live mercury on the walls and cinnabar ore from which the metal is extracted. A chapel in the mine served the miners, dedicated to their patron saint, St Barbara.

ⓐ Kosovelova ulica 3 ⓞ 05 377 1142 ⓞ Tours: 10.00 & 15.00 Mon–Fri, 10.00, 15.00 & 16.00 Sat & Sun

🔺 *Waxwork miners bring the mercury mine to life*

Wild Lake

Follow the Idrija River Canal to Wild Lake, a lush lake fed by a clear karst spring. Following heavy rainfalls, the pressure builds up underground forcing the water up like a geyser, giving the impression that the lake is boiling, despite the fact that the water never rises above a near-constant 10°C. Declared a natural monument by the Slovenian government in 1967, the lake's signboards outline details about native trees, plants and wildlife.

On your stroll to the lake, be sure not to miss seeing the Kamsit – a water wheel that was used to pump water out of flooded mines for almost two centuries. It's located about 3 km (2 miles) to the north, about one-third of the journey from the old town.

CULTURE

Municipal Museum

The town of Idrija made its early fortunes on the back of its two major industries: mercury mining and lace-making. Both traditions are chronicled in detail at this intriguing local museum, which takes up three wings of a hilltop castle surrounding a courtyard.

During the 16th century, Idrija became a key centre of industry following the discovery that mercury could be used to separate gold and silver from rock. Town business boomed as a result and an extensive display dedicated to the heavy metal testifies to its importance to local townspeople.

The ethnographic collection tells the story of the miners who resided here, through various reconstructed rooms that detail their lifestyles through the years. A typical local salary up until the 1980s was double the national average, meaning that many luxuries could be afforded when compared to other communities.

A new exhibition exists on the second floor covering Idrija's modern-day history from the days of Italian occupation during World War I through to the early days of socialism and the birth of Yugoslavia. The massive hammer and sickle that dominates the room once hung over the mine entrance.

Finally there is also a large room outlining local lace-making traditions. Regionally produced lace is still valued and examples are highly sought after by collectors.

ⓐ Prelovčeva ulica 9 ☏ 05 372 6600 ⓦ www.muzej-idrija-cerkno.si
🕒 08.00–18.00 Mon–Fri, 09.00–18.00 Sat & Sun

AFTER DARK

Restaurants

Gostlina Kos £ Žlikrofi is a local speciality that resembles ravioli and is stuffed with bacon, chives and potatoes. This pub dishes up the town's best examples – but you'd better be hungry because it's extraordinarily filling. ⓐ Tomšičeva ulica 4 ☏ 05 372 2030

Pri Škafarju £ While there are tons of menu options, most locals stick to the tasty pizza made in the on-site wood-burning oven.
ⓐ Ulica Svete Barbare 9 ☏ 05 377 1162

ACCOMMODATION

Dijaški Dom Nikolaj Pirnat £ Student dormitory close to the town centre. The multi-bed rooms are only available during the summer months. ⓐ Ulica IX Korpusa 6 ☏ 05 373 4070

Gostišče Barbara ££ Located directly above the entrance to the Anthony Mine Shaft, this six-room property is standard and central.
ⓐ Kosovelova ulica 3 ☏ 05 377 1162

Hotel Kendov Dvorec ££–£££ For total romance, book yourself into the castle hotel located 4 km (2.5 miles) north of town. There are only 12 rooms in this converted family mansion, which dates back to the 14th century. Guests can enjoy the antique 19th-century furnishings and views of the Idrijca Valley. Be sure to book yourself

in for a meal at the hotel's Hana Room. Even if you aren't staying here, it's worth the trip. ⓐ Spodnja Idrija ⓣ 05 372 5100 ⓦ www.kendov-dvorec.com

POTOROŽ AND THE SLOVENIAN COAST

Love it or hate it, Potorož is the seaside town of choice in Slovenia. Visitors would be forgiven for making the obvious comparisons to Blackpool or Benidorm, possibly confused by the tacky high-rise developments that line the coast – but locals love the place and flock to its sandy beaches whenever warm weather strikes.

A resort has existed at this location for centuries, as visitors have been drawn by the (supposedly) healing waters of its local spas. While there isn't much visually to speak of today, the spas remain active and are firmly aimed at the working classes of the country, meaning they are heavy on function and light on form.

For a more graceful seaside holiday, go instead to the beautiful Venetian-era town of Piran just a few kilometres further up the coast. Not only is this village more visually striking, it also attracts Slovenia's glitterati, due to its truly unspoilt atmosphere. During the summer months, buses leave regularly from Ljubljana station. The E70 motorway takes drivers directly to the coastal resorts, but be warned that warm weekends can see legendarily bad traffic.

▶ *The idyllic streets of Idrija*

Southern Slovenia

South of Ljubljana is a region of natural beauty, dotted with few towns and even fewer tourists. The main attractions are centred around the town of Postojna. However, the rolling hills and thick forests hold secret treasures in the form of beautiful rock formations, hidden monasteries, castles, spas, vineyards and delightful valleys carved out by ancient rivers. Known for its fruit-growing, folk traditions abound here, and celebrations can be found in various towns on weekends throughout the summer.

Cycling, hiking and camping possibilities are many, and the various towns offer great wine-tasting options for fans of the locally produced light red wine. Getting around this region is difficult, especially outside the main administrative centres. Bus and train services are limited, making a car a necessity if this region is top of your itinerary.

POSTOJNA

The town of Postojna isn't of particular interest, but serves as the jumping-off point for one of Slovenia's most visited sights – the Postojna Caves. Highly forgettable, the town serves as the administrative centre for the region and should be avoided if visits to the caves and castle aren't in your plans. A stay of a day or two will cover all the sights with plenty of time to spare. Buses depart Ljubljana every half-hour to Postojna as they travel their way to the coast. The town is also on the main train line to Trieste. The journey takes about an hour. To drive, take the A1/E61/E70 motorway.

SIGHTS & ATTRACTIONS

Postojna Caves

Over 19 km (12 miles) of tunnels, chambers and passages make up the Postojna Cave system, which lies under a limestone plateau. The sight of forest-like stalagmites and stalactites is inspiring, formed by millions of years of erosion and rainfall seeping through the limestone ceiling.

⬥ *Take a cave tour to see ancient stalactites*

Signatures carved into the walls date from 1213, but only became famous following a visit by Emperor Franz Ferdinand in 1819. An electric train has since been installed, taking visitors 4 km (2.5 miles) into the heart of the system.

Cave tours can be extremely popular during summer. Try to go on either the first or last tour of the day to avoid the crowds, and be sure to dress warmly as the interior can get quite cold.

During the tour, the main attraction, in addition to the various chambers and formations, is a tank containing *Proteus anguinus* – the largest cave-dwelling vertebrate in the world. A bizarre-looking creature, it was originally mistaken for a dragon when first discovered by locals many centuries ago. ⓐ Jamska cesta 30 ⓣ 05 700 0100 ⓦ www.postojna-cave.com ⓛ Tours: 09.00–18.00, hourly May–Sept; 10.00, 12.00, 14.00 & 16.00 Mon–Sun Mar; 10.00, 12.00, 14.00, 16.00 Mon–Fri, 10.00–17.00 Sat & Sun hourly Apr & Oct; 10.00, 14.00 Mon–Fri, 10.00, 12.00, 14.00, 16.00 Sat & Sun Nov–Feb

Predjama Castle

If not for the Postojna Caves, the Predjama Castle would easily be the most impressive sight in the region. Located 9 km (5.6 miles) north of Postojna town, the castle is located in the mouth of a cavern halfway up a 123 m (404 ft) cliff. The result is high drama.

While a castle has stood here since the 12th century, the present structure dates from the 16th century and includes a number of styles from Romanesque to Gothic.

ⓞ *The 'castle in the rock' at Predjama*

The interiors of the castle are far less inspiring than the exterior, filled with eight reconstructed museum rooms. Be sure to examine the drawbridge, dungeon and secret passage entrance.

Of greater interest are the caves below the castle. Only 900 m (2,953 ft) are available for exploration, and as the path is only partially constructed and there is no lighting installed, boots and a torch are required. ❸ Predjamski Grad ❶ 05 751 6015 ⓦ www.postojna-cave.com ⓛ June–Aug 09.00–19.00 Mon–Sun; May & Sept 09.00–18.00, daily; Mar, Apr & Oct 10.00–17.00 Mon–Sun; Nov–Feb 10.00–16.00 Tues–Fri, until 17.00 Sat & Sun

LAKE CERKNICA

Located east of Postojna is Lake Cerknica, a 'disappearing' lake that has been written about since the days of the Greek Empire. The lake is only a lake during short periods, created when the area floods during the autumn and spring. Fed by waters from the plateaus to the east and mountains to the west, the lake can be created over the course of just a few days. At its largest, it can grow to 10 km (6 miles) in length and 5 km (3 miles) wide. As the drier summer months approach, the lake slowly disappears into the sinkholes and potholes on which the lake is located, taking as long as three to four weeks to finally be erased until the next rainy season. For a better understanding of how the lake works, include a visit to the Museum of Lake Cerknica in the town of Dolenje Jezero. Exhibits include live bird recordings, a 25-minute slide show of lake images and a model of local canoes, used until as recently as 1970 to transport livestock across the water. ❸ Dolenje jezero 1e ❶ 01 709 4053 ⓦ www.jezerski-hram.si ⓛ 15.00 Sat only. Tours at other times can be arranged by calling in advance.

TAKING A BREAK

Pizzeria Minutka £ Local pizzeria with an outdoor terrace popular with locals. ⓐ Ljubljanska cesta 14 ⓣ 05 720 3625

AFTER DARK

Restaurants
Jadran ££ Centrally located 'old-fashioned' eatery that's strong on fish dishes. ⓐ Titov trg 1 ⓣ 05 720 3900

Restavracija Jamska ££ Located at the entrance to the caves and featuring a selection of eight set menus. The 1920s-style building provides pleasant surroundings. ⓐ Jamska cesta 28 ⓣ 05 700 0181

Bars, clubs & discos
Bar Bor There aren't that many party options in this sleepy town. Bar Bor stands out due to its central location. ⓐ Tržaška cesta 4a ⓣ 05 726 4230

ACCOMMODATION

Hotel Jama £–££ This mid-to-large hotel was recently renovated, and is convenient only if explorations of Postojna Caves are a top priority. Just 200 m (656 ft) southeast of the cave entrance, it's a bit of a trek to the town centre. ⓐ Jamska cesta 28 ⓣ 05 728 2400 ⓦ www.postojna-cave.com

Hotel Kras ££ As the only hotel in the town centre, this property leaves a lot to be desired. A renovation is much-needed – but with

no competition, don't expect one anytime soon. ⓐ Tržaška cesta 1
ⓣ 05 726 4071 ⓦ www.hotel-kras.com

Novo Mesto

The town of Novo Mesto is the largest in southeast Slovenia and
has been an important cultural and economic centre since the
Middle Ages. The region has been continuously settled since the

🔺 *Mesmerising sculptures on the Chapter Church of St Nicholas*

Bronze Age, and numerous archaeological sites attest to this fact. Today, it has a strong industrial base, housing both pharmaceutical and automotive factories. While sights are limited, it's a convenient jumping-off point for explorations of the surrounding hills and spas – and the museum with its extensive collection of artefacts is fascinating for fans of the Bronze and Middle Ages. Ten buses and 15 trains serve Novo Mesto from Ljubljana every day, each taking about an hour. By car, take the E70/H1 motorway towards Croatia. Novo Mesto is located halfway between Ljubljana and Zagreb.

SIGHTS & ATTRACTIONS

Chapter Church of St Nicholas

This church is the town's oldest monument, designed using a mish-mash of Gothic, neo-Gothic and baroque architectural elements. While the 15th-century presbytery is the most celebrated feature of the church, there are also a number of intriguing works of art, including a Tintoretto – one of only two in the entire country.

ⓐ Kapiteljski hrib ⓒ Hours vary; keys can be obtained from the Provost's House ⓐ Kapiteljska ulica 1

Glavni Trg

The main square of the old town is home to the neo-Renaissance city hall, and was once the address of choice for craftsmen and merchants. Other buildings located nearby include St Leonard's Franciscan church, visible due to its classy yellow gabled façade, the adjoining monastery and Jakac House, with its collection of sketches and drawings created by Slovenian artist Božidar Jakac.

CULTURE

Dolenjska Museum

Located in a building that once housed the Knights of the Teutonic Order, this large museum holds a strong collection of archaeological finds that were unearthed during the late 1960s. The most important artefact is the Hallstatt helmet, dating from 800 BC, with two axe blows carved into the top. Other exhibits examine recent and ethnographic history, with a strong focus on World War II partisans.

ⓐ Muzejska ulica 7 ⓣ 07 373 1130 ⓦ www.dolmuzej.com
ⓛ 08.00–17.00 Tues–Fri, 10.00–17.00 Sat, 10.00–13.00 Sun Apr–Sept; 08.00–16.00 Mon–Fri, 09.00–13.00 Sat, 09.00–12.00 Sun Oct–Mar

TAKING A BREAK

Picerija Tratnik Slovenia loves its pizzerias and Novo Mesto is no exception. This eatery is the most central one to enjoy a slice or two.
ⓐ Glavni trg 11 ⓣ 07 332 1551

AFTER DARK

Restaurants

Restavracija Breg £–££ Back in its day, this restaurant was a favoured dining spot for Slovenia's artists and intelligentsia. Savvy bohemians still come here to enjoy the hearty local specialities, including bottles of the light Slovenian red wine produced in the region. In warmer months, meals can be enjoyed in the garden.
ⓐ Cvelbarjeva ulica 9 ⓣ 07 332 1269

Tsing Tao £–££ Chinese cuisine in a small Slovenian town? Surprisingly, it's actually pretty good. Dishes are simple and don't stray far from the usual options. ⓐ Dilančeva ulica 7 ⓣ 07 332 4388

Bars, clubs & discos
Kapucinka Nice place for a late-night pint or two. Friendly and welcoming. ⓐ Rozmanova ulica 21 ⓣ 07 332 3767

Pri Slonu Cosy pub popular with the local student and artist crowd. Less raucous than most. ⓐ Rozmanova ulica 22 ⓣ 07 332 1495

Cinemas & theatres
House of Culture This local cinema offers screenings every night at 20.00 and sponsors occasional live music and theatre performances. ⓐ Prešernov trg 3 ⓣ 07 332 1214

ACCOMMODATION

Apartmaji in Sobe Ravbar £ While these five guesthouses are inconveniently located south of the river, the family-run atmosphere and leafy location more than make up for it. ⓐ Smrečnikova ulica 15–17 ⓣ 07 373 0680

Hotel Krka ££ This central hotel caters for business travellers. As such, most are designed with function more than form in mind. ⓐ Novi trg 1 ⓣ 07 394 2100 ⓦ www.krka.si

Eastern Slovenia

While this area doesn't boast the well-known attractions and sights west of Ljubljana, it does have quaint countryside towns and picture-perfect nature spots. In spring and summer, the region comes into its own with a number of music, dance and folk festivals.

Maribor and Celje (the second- and third-largest cities in Slovenia) provide the economic backbone for the region, but pale sight-wise to the more appealing tourist spots of the rural respites that surround them, specifically the town of Ptuj.

Eastern Slovenia is well known for its wine producing and natural spas. Spend your days soaking in the healing waters and your nights imbibing the various vintages.

⬤ *Sculpture in the castle at Maribor*

Maribor

Slovenia's second-largest city, it feels like a small town when compared with the capital. The old Austrianate centre has a number of churches and squares and it's a great jumping-off point for Slovenian nature tours. To the north lie great wineries, while hiking and camping opportunities abound to the south at the Pohorje Massif.

Up to eight buses service Maribor from Ljubljana every day, with additional daily services available to Austria, Germany and Croatia. Maribor is also on the main train line linking Celje with Vienna and Graz. From Ljubljana, the journey time is 1¾hrs by express train. By car from Ljubljana, take motorway E57/A1.

SIGHTS & ATTRACTIONS

Cathedral

The dominant building on Slomškov trg is the 13th-century Cathedral dedicated to St John the Baptist. Architectural styles range from Romanesque to neo-Gothic.

🅐 Slomškov trg

Maribor Castle

Located on the northeast corner of Maribor's main Old Town square, this castle was built in the 15th century over a medieval fortress. The interiors combine baroque and rococo features.

🅐 Grajski trg 2 ☎ 02 228 3551 🕘 09.00–17.00 Tues–Sat, 10.00–14.00 Sun Apr–Dec

Synagogue

To the west of the city's old water tower is a series of steps leading to Židovska ulica (Jewish Street) and the city's Jewish district. In addition to the square Jewish Tower, which now holds a photo gallery, is the restored 15th-century synagogue.

ⓐ Židovska ulica 4 ⓣ 02 252 7836 ⓒ 07.30–14.30 Mon–Fri

CULTURE

Maribor Regional Museum

The ground floor features archaeological, clothing and ethnographic exhibits, while the second floor offers Greek, Roman and Jewish artefacts, in addition to examples of local arts and crafts.

ⓐ Pokrajinski Muzej Maribor, Maribor Castle, Grajski trg 2
ⓣ 02 228 3551 ⓦ www.pmuzej-mb.si ⓒ 09.00–17.00 Tues–Sat, 10.00–14.00 Sun Apr–Dec

TAKING A BREAK

Gledališka Kavarna £ Bohemians, artists and the local gay crowd congregate at this 'Theatre Café' located next to the Slovenian National Theatre. ⓐ Slovenska ulica 2 ⓣ 02 252 3720

AFTER DARK

Restaurants

Gotišče Pri Treh Ribnikih ££ Also known as the 'Inn of the Three Fishponds', this restaurant is a country-style eatery in the middle of City Park. Dishes are heavy and filling, featuring dumplings and plenty of pork. ⓐ Ribniška ulica 3 ⓣ 02 234 4170

Bars, clubs & discos

Jazz Club Satchmo Live jazz club located in the cellar of the Fine Arts Gallery. ⓐ Strossmayerjeva ulica 6 ⓣ 02 250 2150

Patrick's Pub Lively and authentic-feeling place to quench your thirst. Attracts a lively crowd. ⓐ Poštna ulica 10 ⓣ 02 251 1805

Cinemas & theatres

Maribor Puppet Theatre Year-round puppet performances for both children and adults. ⓐ Ratovški trg 2 ⓣ 02 228 1970 ⓦ www.lg-mb.si ⓛ Opening times vary; check listings

Slovenian National Theatre Maribor Ballet, theatre and opera performances. ⓐ Slovenska ulica 27 ⓣ 02 250 6100 ⓦ www.sng-mb.si ⓛ Box office: 10.00–15.00 Mon–Fri, until 13.00 Sat and 2 hours before each performance

ACCOMMODATION

Uni Hotel £ This central 'residence hotel' houses professors and students during the academic year, but opens up to all during school holidays. Well priced and located. ⓐ Gosposka ulica 30 ⓣ 02 250 6700 ⓦ www.termemb.si

Orel Hotel £–££ For location, this hotel can't be beaten – but it needs a lick of paint. ⓐ Grajski trg 3a ⓣ 02 250 6700 ⓦ www.termemb.si

Hotel Piramida ££ Maribor's only four-star hotel is a former tourist hotel with a few superficial alterations. ⓐ Ulica Heroja Šlandra 10 ⓣ 02 233 4400 ⓦ www.termemb.si

CELJE

This industrial city has been around since Roman times. The Old Town has a number of buildings of interest to architecture buffs, such as Krekov trg with the neo-Gothic Celje Hall, a medieval defence tower and a Water Tower; Slomškov trg's 14th-century Abbey Church of St Daniel; Glavni trg, which is considered to be the heart of the Old Town; and Breg, a street on the south bank of the Savinja River leading to the Capuchin Church of St Cecilia.

Celje can be reached either by hourly train or bus services from Ljubljana, taking about 1¼ hours to complete the journey. If you are driving, take the E57/A1 motorway directly to the city.

SIGHTS & ATTRACTIONS

Šempeter

This town, 12 km (7.5 miles) west of Celje, houses a Roman necropolis that was reconstructed between 1952 and 1966.

ⓐ Rimska Nekropola ⓣ 03 700 2056 ⓦ www.td-sempeter.si
ⓛ 10.00–18.00 Mon–Sun Apr–Sept, 10.00–16.00 Sat & Sun Oct

Stari Grad Celje (Celje Old Castle)

This 13th-century castle is the largest fortress in Slovenia. Located 2 km (1 mile) southeast of the Old Town, it sits high on an escarpment overlooking the region.

ⓐ Cesta na Grad ⓣ 03 548 3144 ⓛ 09.00–21.00 Mon–Sun May–Sept; 09.00–19.00 Mon–Sun Apr & Oct; 10.00–17.00 Mon–Sun Nov–Mar

CULTURE

Celje Regional Museum

Skulls of 18 of its former counts are displayed in glass cabinets, but the main attraction is a ceiling known as the Celjski Strop (Celje Ceiling), which was painted in the early 17th century by an anonymous Polish artist.

🅐 Pokrjinski Muzej Celje 🅣 03 428 0950 🅛 10.00–18.00 Tues–Sun

Museum of Recent History

Located in the former town-hall building, this museum chronicles Celje from the late 19th century to the present day.

🅐 Muzej Novejše Zgodovine Celje 🅣 03 422 6410 🅛 10.00–18.00 Mon–Fri; 09.00–12.00 Sat; 14.00–18.00 Sun

TAKING A BREAK

Gostilnica Tartini £ Attractive lunch stop convenient for those visiting the museum. Typical, café-style sandwiches and local dishes.
🅐 Glavni trg 12 🅣 03 492 4450

AFTER DARK

Restaurants
Gostilna Amerika £ Huge dishes of Southern Balkan specialities including vegetable stews and skewered meats.
🅐 Mariborska cesta 79

Istrska Konoba ££ Probably Celje's fanciest restaurant. Also known as the 'Istrian Cellar', the interiors were designed by karst artist Lojze

Spacal. The doors and windows feature stunning examples of stained glass. ⓐ Gledališka ulica 7 ⓣ 03 548 4611

Bars, clubs & discos
Branibor Pub Live music and jazz pub. Good for a chilled evening out. ⓐ Satnetova ulica 27 ⓣ 03 492 4144

Maverick Pub For something a little more action-packed, head to this pub's outdoor terrace during the summer months.
ⓐ Ljubljanska cesta 7

Cinemas & theatres
Slovenski Ljudsko Gledališče (Slovenian People's Theatre)
Considered one of the best professional theatres in Slovenia, this venue hosts the Days of Comedy festival in February. Closed through

⬥ *Ptuj overlooks the Drava River*

much of July and August. ⓐ Gledališka ulica 5 ⓛ Box office:
09.00–11.00, 17.00–19.00 Mon–Fri, also 60 minutes prior to
each performance

ACCOMMODATION

Dijaški Dom (Student Dorm) £ Cheap and cheerful dorm-style
rooms, just 300 m (985 ft) from the main tourist office. Only
available July and August. ⓐ Ljubljanska 21 ⓣ 03 426 6600

Hotel Evropa ££ Clean, comfortable and modern rooms conveniently
located close to the train station. ⓐ Krekov trg 4 ⓣ 03 426 9000
ⓦ www.hotel-evropa.si

Turška Mačka ££ Also known as the 'Turkish Cat', this hotel is the
cheapest in town (other than the student accommodation). Rooms
are slightly gloomy but serviceable. ⓐ Gledališka ulica 7 ⓣ 03 548
4611 ⓦ www.majolka.si

PTUJ

Equal to Ljubljana in historical importance, the town of Ptuj is one of
Slovenia's oldest towns. The compact medieval core is dominated by
the hilltop castle northwest of the centre.

From Ljubljana, travel to Maribor and then take one of the regular
weekday bus services. On weekends, travel is limited, so plan in
advance. Bus and train journeys may include a change in Maribor and
take three hours to reach the town. Drivers should follow the E57/A1
motorway in the direction of Maribor, and exit at Slovenska Bistrica,
following signs to Ptuj.

SIGHTS & ATTRACTIONS

Drava Tower
Built in the 16th century, the Renaissance water tower was built to help defend the town from the Turks. Today, it houses a gallery dedicated to the works of graphic artist France Mihelič.
ⓐ Dracska ulica 4 🕐 10.00–13.00 & 16.00–19.00 Tues–Fri

Minorite Monastery
This massive working monastery was built in the 13th century and escaped the Habsburg religious dissolution edicts. On the first floor is a summer refectory featuring stucco work, and ceiling paintings chronicling the lives of St Peter and St Paul. There is also a stunning library of 5,000 manuscripts including an original copy of the New Testament from the mid-16th century.

The northern side of the monastery is dominated by the Church of Ss Peter & Paul – once considered to be the finest example of Gothic architecture in Slovenia.
ⓐ Minoritski trg 1 ☎ 02 771 3091 🕐 Open by appointment only

Ptuj Castle
Built in the early 12th century, it has a fascinating collection of musical instruments dating back to the 17th century.

The first floor features period rooms of portraits, weapons, furniture and tapestries. The top floor is dedicated to Gothic art.
ⓐ Na Gradu 1 ☎ 02 748 0260 🕐 09.00–17.00 Mon–Sun mid-Oct–May; 09.00–18.00 Mon–Sun June, Sept–mid-Oct; 09.00–18.00 Mon–Fri, 09.00–20.00 Sat & Sun July & Aug

Slovenski Trg

Considered the heart of Ptuj, this street houses the bulk of the town's most celebrated buildings. Structures to check out include the local theatre, a Roman 'Orpheus Monument' dating from the 2nd century AD and a tower built in the 16th century that acted as a watchtower.

CULTURE

Ptuj Regional Museum

Housed in the former Dominican Monastery inside Ptuj Castle, the museum's highlights include lapidary and archaeological exhibits.
ⓐ Muzejski trg 1 ⓣ 02 787 9230 ⓛ 09.00–17.00 Mon–Sun mid-Oct–May; 09.00–18.00 Mon–Sun June, Sept–mid-Oct; 09.00–18.00 Mon–Fri, until 20.00 Sat & Sun July & Aug

TAKING A BREAK

Grajska Kavarna £ Great café serving light drinks and snacks. A nice place for a lunch or coffee break. ⓐ Na Gradu 1 ⓣ 02 787 9230

AFTER DARK

Restaurants

Ribič £–££ Delightful fish restaurant that offers local river catches, including delicious trout and seafood soup. ⓐ Dravska ulica 9
ⓣ 02 749 0635

Bars, clubs & discos
Café Evropa By day, this café is a popular locale for a pint and a pizza. On weekends it becomes the hottest club in town. ⓐ Mestni trg 2 ⓣ 02 787 6570

Teater Kamra Caffè On weekdays, this café attracts a bohemian crowd. Weekends offer live music, including rock, folk and jazz. ⓐ Prešernova ulica 6 ⓣ 02 787 7455

Cinemas & theatres
Kino Ptuj Art and mainstream movies shown at a jewel-like Art Deco filmhouse. ⓐ Cvetkov trg 3 ⓣ 02 748 1810

ACCOMMODATION

Dijaški Dom Ptuj £ Local branch of Hostelling International. Thirteen rooms are available, offering between two and six beds per room. ⓐ Osojnikova cesta 9 ⓣ 02 771 0814

Hotel Poetovio Ptuj £–££ Intimate hotel featuring bright rooms. Drawbacks include its location above a rather noisy casino and slightly dodgy location near the train and bus stations. ⓐ Vinarski trg 5 ⓣ 02 779 8201 ⓦ www.memoria.si

Garni Hotel Mitra ££–£££ Large rooms and a superb location make this hotel the best option in town. ⓐ Prešernova ulica 6 ⓣ 02 787 7455

● *Getting around in Slovenia is not a problem*

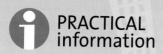

Directory

GETTING THERE
By air

For a short stay, those coming from the UK will find flying the quickest and most convenient way to get to Ljubljana. The main entry point for scheduled flights into Slovenia is Brnik Airport, which is served by the Slovenian flag carrier, ADRIA, a limited number of mostly Eastern European airlines and low-cost carrier easyJet. Located 27 km (17 miles) northwest of the city, it's a basic facility providing exchange services, a hotel booking facility, car rental services, an ATM... and not much else. Travellers from the US will need to change planes in a European hub (most likely London, Paris or Munich) before reaching their final destination, as there are no non-stop services from North America. The average flying time from London is 2 hrs, or 9 hrs from New York including connections. Two other airports, Maribor and Portorož, are rarely used by foreign travellers. See also page 48 for more details on airports.

Many people are aware that air travel emits CO_2, which contributes to climate change. You may be interested in the possibility of lessening the environmental impact of your flight through the charity Climate Care, which offsets your CO_2 by funding environmental projects around the world. Visit www.climatecare.org

By rail

A second-class ticket to Slovenia, incorporating Eurostar, will cost around £260 from London Waterloo. The journey will involve two train changes – once in Paris and again in Venice. The total journey time is approximately 12–16 hours, depending on connections. The monthly *Thomas Cook European Rail Timetable* has up-to-date schedules for European international and domestic train services.

Eurostar reservations ⓣ (UK) 08705 186 186 ⓦ www.eurostar.com
Thomas Cook European Rail Timetable ⓣ (UK) 01733 416 477
(USA) 1 800 322 3834 ⓦ www.thomascookpublishing.com

By road

Roads in Slovenia are well maintained, but on the narrow side. While the journey from London is pleasant, it is on the long side at 1,500 km (932 miles) in length. If you are considering extensive travel around Slovenia, then it can be a good option.

Once across the channel, the most direct route is via Brussels, Stuttgart, Munich and Salzburg, before crossing into Slovenia at the Karavanke Tunnel. Journey time is approximately 30 hours without stops.

The country has a high level of car ownership, but roads remain relatively traffic-free. Snarls can occur in Ljubljana city centre, but they are nothing when compared to the problems of larger European capitals. Distances between destinations in Slovenia tend to be very short. Heavy snowfall can cause problems, especially in the Julian Alps. To drive in Slovenia, a driving licence and third-party insurance are required.

Slovenian traffic drives on the right and the speed limit is 130 kph (80 mph) on motorways, 100 kph (60 mph) on secondary or tertiary roads, and 50 kph (30 mph) in cities and towns. The most important road rules to adhere to while in the country are the prohibition against sounding the horn in built-up areas (unless in order to avoid an accident), and using a mobile phone while driving. Seatbelt use is compulsory, a triangular breakdown sign must be kept in the car at all times, and dipped headlights must be switched on at all times throughout the day.

By bus

A bus journey from the UK is not advised. Eurolines, the main bus company operating European coaches from London, does not operate services to Ljubljana. There is, however, a service from London to Maribor in eastern Slovenia. The journey time is 30 hours and involves a change in Frankfurt. A standard return fare is £140.

Eurolines ☎ 0870 514 3219 Ⓦ www.eurolines.co.uk

ENTRY FORMALITIES
Visa requirements

Visitors to Slovenia who are citizens of the UK, Ireland, Australia, the US, Canada, Israel or Japan will need a passport, but not a visa, for stays of up to 90 days. South African nationals do require a visa. If you are travelling from other countries, you may need a visa and it is best to check before you leave home.

Customs

Customs controls and inspections for visitors from EU countries are either cursory or nonexistent. An exception is when travelling with pets, as inspectors will be vigilant when examining rabies and vaccination certificates. A certificate of health for your pet must not be more than ten days old. Visitors can bring in, or take out, goods without restrictions on quantity or value, as long as these goods are for personal use only.

Other items that are duty-free include: 200 cigarettes (100 cigarillos, 50 cigars or 150 g of tobacco), 2 l of wine and 1 l of spirits, and 50 g of perfume. The import or export of more than 3,000,000 SIT is forbidden unless permission has been obtained from the Bank of Slovenia.

As entry requirements and customs regulations are subject to change, you should always check the current situation with your local travel agent, airline or a Slovenian embassy or consulate before you leave.

MONEY

The currency in Slovenia is the tolar (sounds like dollar), abbreviated as SIT. Theoretically, the tolar is divided into 100 stotinov, but these aluminium coins are so worthless they are rarely distributed. Coin denominations are: 1 tolar, 2 tolar, 5 tolar, 10 tolar, 20 tolar and 50 tolar. Paper money comes in larger denominations of 10, 20, 50, 100,

🔺 Bus routes connect the city to the countryside

200, 500 and 1000 SIT. You can withdraw money from ATMs at many Slovenian banks. There are moves to adopt the euro, though this is not expected to occur until 2007 at the earliest. The most widely accepted credit cards are MasterCard, American Express and Visa. Diner's Club is less useful. Many smaller businesses, including some restaurants, taverns, hotels and most market stalls, do not accept credit-card payment. This is especially true outside Ljubljana and the main tourist destinations. It is advisable always to carry a small amount of cash to cover your day's purchases.

HEALTH, SAFETY & CRIME

It is not necessary to take any special health precautions while travelling in Slovenia. Tap water is safe to drink, but do not drink any water from surrounding lakes or rivers. Many Slovenians prefer bottled mineral water.

If you are going to do a lot of walking in forested areas, it is necessary to be careful of ticks. These blood-sucking parasites can transmit dangerous viral infections, along with various bacterial diseases. A good deterrent is the insecticide permethrin, sprinkled over your clothes. It is also wise to avoid walking through long grass with bare legs. In any case, after a walk always check your body for ticks. If you find one, remove it immediately with a pair of tick tweezers. These can be bought at pharmacies. Ask how to use them when buying. If a rash develops from a bite, consult a doctor immediately.

Pharmacies (or *lekarna*) are present throughout Ljubljana and most other Slovenian communities. Opening hours are usually from 07.00 to 19.00. A sign in the door will notify you as to the location of the nearest 24-hour pharmacy, should you need something in an emergency. Slovenian pharmacists are always well stocked and staff can provide expert advice.

Slovenian health care is of a good standard, but it is not free. EU citizens are entitled to reduced-cost, sometimes free, medical treatment that becomes necessary while travelling in Slovenia, on presentation of their European Health Insurance Card (EHIC; www. ehic.org.uk). In most cases your travel insurance should provide the coverage you need.

As in any other big cities, crime is a fact of life in Ljubljana. Petty theft (bag-snatching, pickpocketing) is the most common form of trouble; however, you are unlikely to experience violence or assault. Never leave valuables lying openly in your car, and always lock it. Strolling around the inner city at night is fairly safe, but avoid dimly lit streets. Your hotel will warn you about particularly dangerous or unwelcoming areas – but there really are very few.

When using public transport or walking on the street, carry your wallet in your front pocket, keep bags closed at all times, never leave valuables on the ground when you are seated at a table and always wear camera bags and purses crossed over your chest.

For emergency numbers, see 'Emergencies' on page 156.

OPENING HOURS

Most shops and department stores open Monday to Friday 08.00– 19.00, until 13.00 on Saturdays. Stores generally do not open on Sundays or public holidays. Weekend opening hours are not conducive to weekend short-breakers with a love of retail therapy. If you really want to shop, the BTC City mall located 3 km (2 miles) from the city centre stays open until 20.00 on Saturdays, and from 08.00–13.00 on Sundays. Local pressure groups are campaigning to stop this practice, so be sure to check in advance. Banks open Monday to Friday 08.00– 16.00 or 17.00, with a one- or two-hour lunch break at some point during the day. Major branches will also open from 08.00–13.00 on Saturdays.

Cultural institutions close for one day per week – usually Mondays. Standard hours are 10.00–18.00 from April–October. During the winter months, this schedule may be shortened, or may be reduced to weekends only.

Usual post office opening hours are 08.00-19.00 Monday to Friday and Saturday 08.00–12.00 or 13.00.

TOILETS

Slovenia isn't exactly blessed with copious public lavatory facilities. When in doubt, head for the nearest train station, shopping centre or department store. Standards of hygiene are usually pretty good, but you will need to pay anything from 30 to 50 SIT for the pleasure. Alternatively, try asking at one of the local cafés or bars. You may sometimes be expected to make a token purchase of coffee or water for the experience.

CHILDREN

Slovenia is generally a child-friendly place and no special health precautions need be taken for children, other than the above. Most restaurants, including the fanciful ones, welcome children. In some of the more 'neighbourhood' restaurants, there is usually a kids' menu. High chairs and cots come as standard at most dining establishments and hotels, but it's wise to book ahead.

Nappies and other baby necessities are readily obtained from supermarkets, and *lekarna* (pharmacies). Remember that weekend opening hours are extremely limited so be sure to purchase all your weekend baby needs in advance.

There are plenty of attractions in and around Ljubljana that will keep the kids occupied, but if the numerous museums and historic sights prove to be a little overwhelming, consider bringing the kids to the

Puppet Theatre or the zoo on Rožnik Hill. Alternatively, take a stroll through the BTC City mall where there are lots of kid-focused diversions.

COMMUNICATIONS
Phones

Coin-operated public phones do not exist. If you want to make a call from one of the more than 4,000 public telephones in Slovenia, you will need a telephone card known as a *telefonska kartika*, or *telekartica* for short. Telephone cards can be bought at any post office and some newsstands. Phonecards cost 700/1,000/1,700/3,500 SIT for 25/50/100/300 units of time. A three-minute local call during peak time (07.00–19.00 weekdays) costs about 19 units. For Western Europe (including the UK), Canada and the USA, this charge would be 126 SIT. Rates are 20 per cent cheaper after 19.00 on weekdays.

Instructions on how to use public telephones are written in English in phone booths for international calls. Otherwise, lift up the receiver, insert the telephone card and dial the number.

When making an international call, dial the international code you require and drop the initial zero of the area code you are ringing. The international dialling code for calls from Slovenia to Australia is 061; to the UK 044; to the Irish Republic 0353; to South Africa 027; to New Zealand 064; and to the USA and Canada 01. The code to dial Slovenia from abroad, after the access code (00 in most countries), is 386. To call Ljubljana from within Slovenia dial 01 and then the number, unless calling within Ljubljana itself when there is no need to dial 01.

Post

Postal services are quick and efficient. There are many post offices throughout the city, but the most convenient locations can be found at Slovenska 32 and trg Osvobodilne fronte 5. Stamps and phonecards can be bought at the post offices and there are rarely any long queues. If you don't find yourself close to a post office, some newsstands also sell both items. Post boxes are yellow. Letters weighing less than 20 g are 107 SIT or 221 SIT for up to 100 g. Postcards cost 83 SIT. The airmail charge on top of all the above amounts is 137 SIT. It is wise to make the investment.

Internet
Internet access is provided by some libraries and internet cafés around the city. The largest and most popular café is:
Cyber Café Xplorer @ Trubarjeva 52 ● 01 439 7270

ELECTRICITY
The standard electrical current is 220 volts. Two-pin adaptors can be purchased at most electrical shops.

TRAVELLERS WITH DISABILITIES
Facilities for visitors with disabilities are generally quite poor in Slovenia. The country has been slow to catch up with the needs of disabled travellers and still has a long way to go. Few locations are well equipped or even have basic facilities, and access to hotels and public buildings is impossible in many cases.

Facilities for visitors with disabilities arriving at the city's main international airport are good, though travellers with special needs should inform their airlines in advance. The new InterCity Slovenije trains between Ljubljana and Maribor have also joined the 21st century in introducing wheelchair facilities, specially adapted toilets, and access ramps to the platforms.

A useful source of advice when in Slovenia is **Zveza Paraplegikov Slovenije** ⓐ Štihova ulica 14 ⓕ 01 432 7138
ⓦ www.zveza-paraplegikov.si

Useful websites include:
ⓦ www.sath.org (US site).
ⓦ www.access-able.com (general advice on worldwide travel).
ⓦ http://travel.guardian.co.uk (UK site offering tips and links for disabled travellers).

FURTHER INFORMATION

Ljubljana's main tourist office is extremely helpful and shares its space with the Slovenian Tourist Board – so you can get information on the entire country in one convenient location. Maps and information are available free of charge in English.

Ljubljana Tourist Information Centre ⓐ Stritarjeva ⓕ 306 1215
ⓦ www.ljubljana.si/en/tourism ⓛ 08.00–21.00 Mon–Sun
June–Sept; 08.00–19.00 Mon–Sun Oct–May

Background reading

The Sonnets of Unhappiness by France Prešeren. Beautiful poetry from the early 19th century by Slovenia's most iconic literary figure.
The City and the Child by Ales Debeljak. Contemporary poetry anthology by a modern-day master.
Slovenia & the Slovenes by Cathie Carmichael and James Gow. Comprehensive exploration of 20th-century Slovenian history, culture, economics and politics.

Useful phrases

Although English is widely spoken in Slovenia, these words and phrases may come in handy. See also the phrases for specific situations in other parts of the book.

English	Slovenian	Approx. pronunciation
BASICS		
Yes	Ja	Ya
No	Ne	Neh
Please	Prosim	Prosseem
Thank you	Hvala	Khvala
Hello	Zdravo	Zdravo
Goodbye	Nasvidenje	Nassveedenyeh
Excuse me	Prosim	Prosseem
Sorry	Oprostite	Oprossteeteh
That's O.K.	V redu je	Oo-reh-doo yeh
To	Do	Do (as in dot)
From	Od	Od
I don't speak Slovenian	Ne govorim slovensko	Neh govoreem slovensko
Do you speak English?	Govorite angleško?	Govoreeteh angleshko?
Good morning	Dobro jutro	Dobro yootro
Good afternoon	Dober dan	Dobber dan
Good evening	Dober večer	Dobber vecher
Good night	Lahko noč	Lakhko noch
My name is ...	Ime mi je ...	Eemeh mee yeh ...
DAYS & TIMES		
Monday	Ponedeljek	Ponedelyek
Tuesday	Torek	Torek
Wednesday	Sreda	Sreda
Thursday	Četrtek	Chetrhtek
Friday	Petek	Petek
Saturday	Sobota	Sobota
Sunday	Nedelja	Nedelya
Morning	Jutro	Yootro
Afternoon	Popoldne	Popohdneh
Evening	Večer	Vecher
Night	Noč	Noch
Yesterday	Včeraj	Oocheray

English	Slovenian	*Approx. pronunciation*
Today	Danes	*Dah-nes*
Tomorrow	Jutri	*Yootree*
What time is it?	Koliko je ura?	*Koleeko yeh oora?*
It is ...	(Ura je) ...	*Oora yeh...*
09.00	Devet	*Devet*
Midday	Poldne	*Pohdne*
Midnight	Polnoč	*Pohnoch*

NUMBERS

One	Ena	*Ena*
Two	Dva	*Dva*
Three	Tri	*Tree*
Four	Štiri	*Shteeree*
Five	Pet	*Pet*
Six	Šest	*Shest*
Seven	Sedem	*Sedem*
Eight	Osem	*Ossem*
Nine	Devet	*Devet*
Ten	Deset	*Desset*
Eleven	Enajst	*Enayst*
Twelve	Dvanajst	*Dvanayst*
Twenty	Dvajset	*Dvayset*
Fifty	Petdeset	*Pedesset*
One hundred	Sto	*Sto*

MONEY

I would like to change these traveller's cheques/this currency	Rad(a) bi zamenjal(a) te potovalne čeke/to valuto	*Rad(a) bee zamenyal(a) teh potovalneh chekeh/to valooto*
Where is the nearest ATM?	Kje je najbližji bankomat?	*Kyeh yeh nuy-blee-zhyee bahn-koh-maht?*
Do you accept traveller's cheques/credit cards?	Sprejemate potovalne čeke/kreditne kartice?	*Spreyemateh potovalneh chekeh/kredeetneh karteetseh?*

SIGNS & NOTICES

Airport	Letališče	*Letaleeshcheh*
Rail station	Železniška postaja	*Zhelezneeshka postaya*
Platform	Peron	*Peron*
Smoking/Non-smoking	Kadilci/Nekadilci	*Kadeeltsee/Nekadeeltsee*
Toilets	Sanitarije	*Saneetareeyeh*
Ladies/Gentlemen	Ženske/Moški	*Zhenskeh/Moshkee*
Entrance/Exit	Vhod/Izhod	*Ookhod/Eezkhod*

Emergencies

EMERGENCY NUMBERS

The numbers for emergency services are as follows:

Ambulance 112
Fire brigade 112
Police 113

HEALTH

The British Embassy has a list of English-speaking doctors; however, most doctors in Ljubljana speak at least the basics. Make sure that you have a European Health Insurance Card (if you are from the EU) and/or private travel insurance.

There is an emergency medical centre ⓐ Bohoričeva 5 ⓣ 01 552 8408 and an emergency dentist ⓐ Kotnikova 36 ⓣ 01 425 4061.

EMERGENCY PHARMACY

Prescription and non-prescription drugs (including aspirin) are only sold at pharmacies (*lekarna*). Most keep standard business hours, which are 08.30–19.00 Mon–Fri and until 13.00 Sat. A list of pharmacies open on Sundays and in the evening should be displayed near the door of every pharmacy.

HOSPITALS

Klinični Centre Ljubljana ⓐ Zaloška 2 ⓣ 01 552 5050.
Ljubljana Hospital ⓐ Bohoričeva 4 ⓣ 01 232 3060.

POLICE

The Slovenian capital is a relatively safe city with a low crime rate. However, sensible precautions should be taken. Take valuables with you whenever you leave your car unattended, cross purse and satchel straps over the body when walking, and keep wallets in the front pocket of trousers. If you do become a victim, report the crime immediately at the central police station ⓐ Trdinova 10 ☎ 01 432 0341.

Lost property

You will need to visit the control police station. If the item was lost on buses, contact the LPP Information Centre ⓐ Celoška 160 ☎ 01 582 2420 during regular office hours. For items lost on trains check with the information counter at Ljubljana station, and for property left in taxis, contact the office of the taxi company you used.

CONSULATES & EMBASSIES

Australian Consulate ⓐ trg Republike 3/XII ☎ 01 425 4252
British Embassy ⓐ trg Republike 3/IV ☎ 01 200 3910.
🌐 www.british-embassy.si
Canadian Consulate ⓐ Miklošičeva 19 ☎ 01 430 3570
Irish Embassy ⓐ Palača Kapitelj, Poljanski nasip 6 ☎ 01 300 8970
New Zealand Consulate ⓐ Verovškova 57 ☎ 01 580 3055
Republic of South Africa Consulate ⓐ Pražakova 4 ☎ 01 200 6300
US Embassy ⓐ Prešernova 31 ☎ 01 200 5500

EMERGENCY PHRASES

Help! Na pomoč! *Na pomoch!*   **Fire!** Gori! *Goree!*
Stop! Stop! *Stop!*

Call an ambulance/a doctor/the police/the fire brigade!
Pokličite rešilca/zdravnika/policijo/gasilce!
Pokleecheeteh resheeltsa/zdrowneeka/poleetseeyo/gaseeltse!

INDEX

The publishers would like to thank the following for supplying the copyright photographs for this book:

Archiv Postojnske jame/Slovenian Tourist Board: page 123; Bobo/Slovenian Tourist Board: page 49; B Kladnik/Slovenian Tourist Board: page 113; Ljubljana Tourist Board: page 67; I Maher/Slovenian Tourist Board: page 59; D Mladenovič/Slovenian Tourist Board: page 46; Pictures Colour Library: pages 31, 99, 138; J Skok/Slovenian Tourist Board: page 43; Meeli Tamm at pbase.com: pages 16 and 64; Meghan Hurst: all other photographs

Copy editor: Jenni Rainford
Proofreader: Janet McCann

Send your thoughts to
books@thomascook.com

- **Found a great bar, club, shop or must-see sight that we don't feature?**
- **Like to tip us off about any information that needs updating?**
- **Want to tell us what you love about this handy little guidebook and more importantly how we can make it even handier?**

Then here's your chance to tell all! Send us ideas, discoveries and recommendations today and then look out for your valuable input in the next edition of this title. As an extra 'thank you' from Thomas Cook Publishing, you'll be automatically entered into our exciting monthly prize draw.

Send an email to the above address (stating the book's title) or write to: CitySpots Project Editor, Thomas Cook Publishing, PO Box 227, The Thomas Cook Business Park, Unit 18, Coningsby Road, Peterborough PE3 8SB, UK.